The Banality of Goodness

The *Erma Konya Kess*
Lives of the Just and Virtuous Series

The University of Notre Dame Press
gratefully acknowledges the generous support of
the estate of Erma Konya Kess
in the publication of this series.

The Banality of Goodness
The Story of Giorgio Perlasca

Enrico Deaglio

English translation by
Gregory Conti

University of Notre Dame Press
Notre Dame   London
1998

The Banality of Goodness
Copyright © 1998 by
University of Notre Dame Press
Notre Dame, IN 46556
All Rights Reserved.
Manufactured in the United States of America.

Originally published 1991 in Italian as *La Banalità del Bene: Storia di Giorgio Perlasca*

Original copyright:
© Giangiacomo Feltrinelli Editore Milano
Prima edizione in "Tempo ritrovato" ottobre 1991
Terza edizione dicembre 1991
ISBN 88-07-07024-3

Library of Congress Cataloging-in-Publication Data

Deaglio, Enrico, 1947-
    [Banalità del bene. English]
    The banality of goodness : the story of Giorgio Perlasca /
Enrico Deaglio : English translation by Gregory Conti.
      P.   cm.   `
    Includes bibliographical references.
    ISBN 0-268-02154-6 (cloth : alk. paper) —
    ISBN 0-268-02151-1 (pbk. : alk. paper)
    1. Jews—Persecutions—Hungary. 2. Perlasca, Giorgio,
1910- . 3. World War, 1939-1945—Jews—Rescue—Hungary.
4. Righteous Gentiles in the Holocaust—Hungary. 5. Holocaust,
Jewish (1939-1945)—Hungary. 6. Hungary—Ethnic relations.
I. Title.
DS135.H9D4313 1998
940.53'18'09439—dc21
                                            98-13290
                                              CIP

∞The paper used in this publication meets the minimum requirements of the
American National Standard for Information Sciences—Permanence of Paper for
Printed Materials, ANSI Z39.48-1984.

Contents

Translator's Note

The first Italian edition of *La Banalità del Bene* was published in October 1991. Fortunately for all of us, Giorgio Perlasca was still living then, which meant not only that the author was able to interview him and gather his first-hand testimony about the events, but that the Italian authorities were able to read the book and officially recognize Perlasca for his good deeds before he died. The book was then published in an economical edition in February 1993, six months after Perlasca's death, and included an epilogue with an account of events between the first and second editions. This translation is based on the second edition.

The book was originally written for an Italian audience, which could be presumed to be familiar with the important events and personalities of twentieth-century Italian history. For this American edition, I have prepared a few notes on some references in the text, references which may not be familiar to most readers. The notes, however, are not essential to understanding the original text, and I have asked that they be printed as endnotes rather than footnotes so as not to disturb the flow of the narrative.

As I was working on the translation, I was often reminded of my father, Eugene A. Conti, who was like Perlasca in so many ways, and of my mother, Genevieve Keally Conti, whose knowledge of and love for the English language have been a constant source of inspiration. The translation is dedicated to them.

Acknowledgments

First of all, to Giorgio Perlasca, for patiently explaining his story to me, clearing up my misunderstandings, and entrusting his diary to me.

Gad Castel, a television director in Tel Aviv, whom I met during Perlasca's award ceremony in Israel, was the first to talk to me about Perlasca. Together with Castel, Gianni Barcelloni, László Elek, Roberto Pistarino, Carlo Degli Esposti and Áron Sipos, I worked on a report for the Italian television show "Mixer" – always a great show to work for – and the latter three and myself were together for an unforgettable visit to Transylvania, memories of which appear here and there throughout the book. Our report for "Mixer," entitled "A Tribute to Giorgio Perlasca," was broadcast on April 30, 1990, and was seen by 4 million viewers.

Dr. Eveline Blitstein Willinger wrote her account of how Perlasca was discovered especially for this book. Signora Vera Bellani served as an indefatigable expert on travel connections between Padua, Budapest, Berlin, Tel Aviv and Washington. The Centro di Documentazione Ebraica Contemporanea (CDEC) in Milan made available to me books and other documents that would otherwise have been impossible to find. I would particularly like to thank Michele Sarfatti for his continuous suggestions.

Information, corroboration and supplementary material were provided by Giorgio Pressburger, Magda Lapedus, Jorge Mezei, Jaime Vandor, Giovanni Cataluccio, Enrico and Maddalena Padoa, Silvia Garani, Settimio Conti, Monsignor Loris Capovilla, Grazia Levi, Fabio Levi, Lisa Foa, Cecilia Brunazzi, Keith Rotman, Sandro Parenzo, Miles Lerman of the Holocaust Memorial Council, Morris Talanski of the Share Zedek Medical Center, Ándor Weiss of the Emanuel Foundation and by my uncle, Renzo Deaglio, who let me use his library.

Judith Bohacz translated documents from Hungarian.

A special thanks to Dr. Adam Juval for his encouragement.

Among the many people who were fascinated by Perlasca's story was my Venetian friend Checco Zotti, the architect of many wonderful exploits, who died in June of 1990. This book is dedicated to Checco.

E.D.
Rome, July 1991

Introduction

This is a story of opportunity. From a certain perspective, the Holocaust itself was an event that offered countless non-Jews innumerable opportunities to do what was human and honorable and, yes, courageous. We know from accounts of the period that all too few men and women chose to act as if listening to their consciences. There were exceptions, however. We think of the German soldier who refused to participate in a firing squad because the only "crime "the intended victims had committed was to have been Jewish, so the soldier had to join the group of condemned. There is the example of Franz Jagersdatter, the Austrian peasant who was put to death because he would not fight in Hitler's immoral war.

Jan Karski, a Polish minor diplomat, under dangerous and painful circumstances was able to alert the Allied forces of the true nature of Nazi internments. German brother and sister Hans and Sophie Scholl were beheaded by the Nazis for their resistance to Nazi policies. Marion Pritchard of the Netherlands saved a Jewish family under extremely hazardous conditions. These names as well as Raoul Wallenberg, Irene Opdyke, Helena Melnyczuk, and others form a list which reflects well on humankind, but it is much too short.

Those who acted honorably in resisting the Nazi evil give the rest of us hope. When each of us is faced with a moral crisis, we can draw strength from the examples of the courageous women and men who went before us. Courage and decency were never dead. Giorgio Perlasca's efforts are a case in point. He saw human beings in trouble, and he acted. There are many reasons for people in such a situation not to get involved. There is the issue of personal safety. What about taking the time and mental energy to reach a decision regarding what to do? How bold can one be in resisting others? While Perlasca may have considered such questions briefly, we know a more overwhelming problem faced him: How to help potential victims?

Perlasca was not an ambassador, not someone used to dealing with foreign dignitaries. He did not even speak the language (Hungarian) of the people in whose nation he performed heroics. There was no suggestion that he was the type of person who could stand up to a Papal Nuncio; that he could contest the Arrow Cross (the anti-Semitic political party); that he could lie about being a Spanish chargé d'affaires; that he was a person who would take great risk *to help strangers.*

In her book on rescuers during the Holocaust, *Conscience and Courage*, Eva Fogelman notes that, faced with the horrors that awaited Jews, Perlasca "instantly volunteered his services to help save Jewish lives." In *The Path of the Righteous*, Mordecai Paldiel (director of the section on Righteous Gentiles at Yad Vashem, the Holocaust memorial center in Jerusalem) credits Perlasca with saving up to a thousand Jewish lives.

What follows is Perlasca's story. Author Enrico Deaglio gives a straight narration. The subject of this story does not need to be romanticized. The actions are powerful enough in their demonstration of courage. And Perlasca was indeed a man of courage. As Winston Churchill said, "Courage is the most important of virtues because it contains all the rest."

Harry James Cargas

"My name is Claudio Principi. I'm calling from Corridonia in the Marche. I'd like to say something about the system for the appointment of lifetime Senators [Senators specially appointed by the President of the Italian Republic]. In my opinion, they should be chosen purposely from among those people who have kept themselves well away from politics. . . . For example, you know who I'm thinking of? I'm thinking of Perlasca, who did all those wonderful things without waiting to be asked. And all over the world there's not a man who doesn't take his hat off to him."

Telephone call from a listener of the Italian radio broadcast "Prima Pagina" [Front Page], June 5, 1991.

I

"What Would You Have Done in My Place?"

"What would you have done in my place?"

One of those pointed questions that demand the listener's complicity. A brief query that begs for understanding by highlighting the speaker's, but above all the listener's, human weakness and fragility. "I was afraid, I ran away. . . . What would you have done in my place?" "Nobody could see me, so I did it. . . . What would you have done in my place?"

But the old man who was putting the question to me wasn't looking for understanding or excuses. On the contrary, he was trying to tell me that it was only natural, that anybody would have had to do what he had done.

It was the autumn of 1989. At the end of September, several Italian newspapers, in the column reserved for "news briefs," had carried a report from Jerusalem about an Italian citizen who had been decorated with prestigious state honors; Signor Giorgio Perlasca, aged 80, who in Budapest, in 1944, had succeeded in saving thousands of Hungarian Jews destined to be sent to concentration camps. A few more lines added that his story had remained untold for almost half a century, and had only been brought to light thanks to the tenacious research of a group of survivors. Another few lines, equally vague, were dedicated to the historical background of the events. Signor Perlasca had passed himself off as a Spanish diplomat, and in this role had succeeded in carrying out his rescue mission.

I was sitting in the small living room of a house in Padua opposite Signor Giorgio Perlasca, who was telling me his story. He had been in the meat-importing business and had been stuck in Budapest after September 8th.[1] Interned together with other Italians, he had escaped and found himself in the Hungarian capital, in the vortex of the final days of the war, alone and without papers. He found refuge in the Spanish embassy, was given a false passport by the Spanish ambassador, and volunteered his services in the humanitarian rescue program then being carried out by Spain, together with the diplomatic delegations of the other neutral countries and the International Red Cross. But then it happened that the Spanish ambassador left Hungary without notice, and Perlasca, who should have been thinking only about saving his own skin, nominated himself as the new Spanish representative to the pro-Nazi Hungarian government. And so, as the authoritative representative of a neutral nation, he secured protection for more than five thousand Hungarian Jews, hiding them in buildings placed under Spanish jurisdiction, negotiating with the Nazis who wanted to deport them, saving them from the bands of Hungarian fanatics who wanted to kill them.

A "great imposter," who then, at the end of the war, returned home and took up his former life, until someone remembered him and tracked him down. A year earlier, he was invited to Budapest where a special session of the Hungarian Parliament greeted him with a standing ovation and conferred on him the Order of the Gold Star. In Jerusalem he planted a carob tree in the "Park of the Just," where thousands of trees commemorate the names of those who came to the aid of the Jews during the years of the Holocaust.

Perlasca lives in a modest apartment on the outskirts of

Padua. The first time I went to see him, he didn't have a telephone. To communicate with him you had to go through his sister, who lived in the building next door. When someone called for Giorgio, she would hang a newspaper out on the terrace with a clothespin so that when Giorgio went out for a walk he would see the signal. Then Giorgio would ring the doorbell, and his sister would come out onto the terrace and tell him who had called. Now he has a telephone, because so many people have been calling that the makeshift system of the newspaper on the terrace couldn't handle the traffic.

"What would you have done in my place?" It would be nice to be able to answer, "I would have done the same thing." It would fit well with the self-image of Italians: *"brava gente"* (good people), people so humane that their humanity needs no rational elaboration but comes from the gut and springs forth – despite all the orders, uniforms and ideologies to the contrary – at the mere sight of someone being humiliated or abused; people endowed with innate theatricality and psychological intuition. One is reminded of Vittorio De Sica in *Generale Della Rovere*, taking on another man's role only because he doesn't want to give in to the Germans and who, for the pleasure of the theater, willingly accepts his own execution. Or of Alberto Sordi and Vittorio Gassman, two unwilling soldiers detached from their unit and on the run during the Great War, who go to their death for friendship, and because they don't want to betray their comrades in arms.[2]

But Giorgio Perlasca's story is much bigger than that. During the war, there were a lot of Italians who helped or "delayed or deflected the course of events" by refusing to commit brutalities, or merely by hiding a file, or making a phone call to warn intended victims. But what Giorgio Perlasca did is unique and astounding. He didn't have a role; he created it for himself. His action was not exhausted in a single gesture; it lasted for months and was accomplished thanks to a talent for organization that produced unhoped-for results in the most dangerous circumstances. But he just didn't have the right stuff to qualify as a hero by contemporary standards. Too much modesty, too little inclination for getting up on stage.

On the shelf in Perlasca's living room, among the various history books and texts about Spain as well as a small personal archive, there was a place for awards and testimonials. The honorary citizenship of Israel, the Order of the Gold Star, cases with various medals sent from different parts of the world. A vase held a cloth rose dipped in gold paint. On its stem was a calling card.

"I've never understood very well what that was," Perlasca told me. "It happened in Jerusalem when I was there for the award. During the ceremony, a woman came up to me with this rose. She gave it to me and then she ran off." The gilded cloth rose was accompanied by a calling card. The inscription, written in English, said, "You saved two members of my family and with them my faith in the human race. Faith that I had begun to lose." Later, watching a film of the award ceremony for Perlasca in Jerusalem, I saw the scene. Perlasca is being embraced by elderly ladies and gentlemen. Two of them show the camera their certificates of protected status issued by the bogus consul and by virtue of which they had been saved. They embrace him again. Perlasca embraces them, without having the least idea of who they are. Then a woman comes over to him, gives him the rose and quickly walks away. In the scenes that follow you can see Perlasca continuing to hold on to the rose, because he doesn't know what to do with it.

The calling card was still attached. Signed Madame Moshe Dak, Jerusalem 92621, plus another address, illegible. We tried looking her up in the telephone book, but that didn't get us anywhere either.

Well then, Signor Perlasca, why did you do it?

> Because I couldn't stand the sight of people being branded like animals. Because I couldn't stand seeing children being killed. That's what I think it was; I don't think I was a hero. When it comes right down to it, I had an opportunity

and I took advantage of it. We have an old proverb that says that it's the opportunity that makes a man a thief. Well, it made me something else. All of a sudden I found that I had become a diplomat, with a lot of people who were depending on me. What do you think I should have done? As it turned out, I think being a fake diplomat was a big help, because I could do things that a real diplomat couldn't do. I mean . . . diplomats are a strange breed. They're not exactly free to do what they want to do. There's etiquette, there are formalities, hierarchies, people to answer to, your career. A lot of things, a lot of constraints that I didn't have.

Judging from the photographs that are left from that period, the role of a diplomat was one for which Perlasca was well-suited. Thirty-four years old, very tall, an elegant demeanor. A decidedly handsome man with light brown hair and blue eyes. He spoke fluent Spanish and could make himself understood in German and Hungarian. He was a man of the world, with a lot of contacts and acquaintances. And, as his wife Nerina says, "Let's come right out and say it, Giorgio was a big, good-looking man, one of those men that appeal to women." (He looks up at the ceiling and smiles.)

And what kind of man were you, Signor Perlasca? Were you perchance also a Jew? Is that why you got so involved?

"No, I was born into a Catholic family, in Como, the second of five children. My father had a law degree, and he was a royal functionary in various cities and towns in the area around Padua. My upbringing taught me some very simple things, like all people were to be considered equal." He thinks for a minute. "Well, more or less equal, because, frankly, I don't see what I have in common with someone who rapes women, or with someone whose profession is exploiting women . . ."

From Como the Perlasca family moved to Trieste, and young Giorgio became an enthusiastic adherent of fascism, in its D'Annunzian version. Because of D'Annunzio, he had a violent argument with one of his school teachers who had condemned

D'Annunzio's escapade in Fiume.[3] "That really cost me. I was expelled for a year from all the schools of the realm. To tell you the truth, I wasn't one to study very hard and, in fact, I didn't even finish at the Technical Institute. I liked to have a good time, spend time with my friends, play soccer. Like a lot of other kids, I read Salgari and dreamed of an adventurous life."[4]

He volunteered to go to Ethiopia, one of the "Black Shirts of the October 28th."[5] In December 1936, he left for Spain as a volunteer in the artillery. "What did I do that for? The political reason was that I too wanted to keep the Mediterranean from becoming a Communist lake. But there was also another aspect to it. If I hadn't gone to Spain I would have had to go to work, as a clerk at the sugar refinery in Pontelungo. And the idea of working in an office just didn't appeal to me. So I left for Spain, one of seventy thousand volunteers, and stayed till it was over. Spain still has a place in my heart. Even today, I love everything about the Spanish – their furious idealism, their pride, their sense of tradition, the language. I picked it up right away. In Budapest they used to say that I spoke perfect Castillian, with a slight Galician accent."

Perlasca picks up a case holding one of his medals. "You see this? A medal I was given by the Padua chapter of ANPI, the National Association of Italian Partisans. I was happy to accept it because I know the members of the association and they're good people. But the funny thing is, though, I'm not an anti-fascist. I stopped being a fascist after the war, but I didn't become an anti-fascist. My story is different. The fascist racial laws of 1938, for example, really bothered me. And I wasn't the only one: I remember how much it was talked about when we got back from Spain. I couldn't understand the discrimination against the Jews. So many of my friends were Jews, in Padua, in Trieste, in Fiume. In Spain, the commander of a battery in my artillery regiment was a Jew, from Rome, by the name of Vito Finzi. Here in Padua, one of the wealthiest men in the city was a supporter of fascism, Baron Treves de' Bonfili. Franco, as everyone knows, was not an anti-Semite. That was my attitude. And then I didn't like the alliance with Hitler's Germany, and I didn't agree with the idea of another war. I had had a lot of respect for Mussolini, but in those years I lost it."

So in September 1939, Perlasca, already a veteran of Ethiopia and Spain, was one of those "recalled to arms" who didn't fit in very well. Named as instructor in "theory and history" for the 20th artillery regiment of Padua, he began to act "out of line," impetuous as he had been years earlier at school, so much so that his superiors decided to get rid of him. "After two months they sent me on unlimited agricultural leave. On the other hand, I had a right to it. I had already fought in two wars."

An unusual route, almost a private road, the one taken by Giorgio Perlasca in reaction to the racial laws. He simply wanted no part of them, thought they were unfair. For him, the Jews were just Italians who professed another religious faith. It was his own conviction; he didn't have any leaders to guide him, because when the "Manifesto della Razza" (The Manifesto of the Race) appeared in all the newspapers, signed by authoritative professors who explained to Italians that they belonged to the "Aryan race" while the inferior "Jewish race" had nothing to do with the national community, a lot of people were astonished, but there was very little public protest. Up to that time, fascism had not shown any particular signs of anti-Semitism, and Italian Jews – 42,000 in all, one of the smallest percentages in Europe – had responded to fascism just like everybody else. Some supported it, others – a few – opposed it, the majority signed up for the party card only when it became necessary.[6]

And yet, unexpected as they were, the racial laws immediately started grinding out progressively more intense discriminatory provisions. Pursuant to decrees enacted at an ever faster pace, foreign Jews were expelled from the country, and Italian Jews were banned from public schools, from the army, from the professions. Mixed marriages were prohibited, and ever greater shares of property were confiscated. It was an aggressive persecution, fed by bureaucratic decrees and increasingly violent attacks in the press until Italian Jews had been deprived of all their rights. Then, in September 1943, they began to be deported to the concentration camps.

The Catholic Church did not oppose the persecution, nor did the monarchy, and there were only rare cases of individual protest in the schools, the courts, the universities and the press. Even the anti-fascist movement itself failed to understand the full significance of the steady, relentless campaign and, among Jews, only five thousand of them realized what was coming in time to leave the country. Many went to Switzerland, and many boarded the ships of the Lloyd Triestino line, bound for destinations all over the world.

Nevertheless, the discomfort felt by our veteran of the Spanish Civil War was not an isolated case. Up to now, however, historians have given only fleeting treatment to "cases of conscience" among card-carrying Fascists, or to resignations from the party, condemned by Mussolini as examples of "pietism." After the war, the "vulgate" of Italian history chose the route of rhetoric and reticence. It was difficult to tell the story of opposition to the racial laws when there really hadn't been any. And as for what became of the victims, of the anonymous or isolated opponents, there wasn't much interest in tracking them down.

Giorgio Perlasca is a handsome, erect old man. Tall and thin, he has a detached demeanor, and when he walks he sways back and forth a little because he drags one leg, a reminder of a stroke he suffered four years ago. He has the same blue eyes and his hair, now white, is cut very short. He takes great pleasure in conversation, he's interested in knowing about others, and he still displays the kindness, the silences and the gallantries of the old "charmeur." He is very precise when he talks about the past, respectful in his judgments of other people. He prefers writing letters to talking on the phone and, when he has to travel, he goes by train and knows how to choose the good ones. Other than that, he has the most peaceful life one can imagine: history books, a walk each morning to the local bar "to see the guys playing cards," an occasional cigarette hidden, more or less, from his wife, and a lot of time playing with his grandson Riccardo.

"It's odd that all of this should happen to me now. . . . It's strange because, when I came back, I tried to tell the story, but it seemed like nobody believed it. It probably wasn't interesting, or maybe it just seemed like an exaggeration. You know what my only connection was to Budapest in those years? An Italian acquaintance of mine whose car I asked to borrow in the last days of the siege. The car got shot up by a machine gun, and he came all the way to Trieste to ask for damages. . . . But then again, that was part of our agreement. At that time, after the war, I was living in Trieste and had become a leader of the Uomo Qualunque Party and also a representative of the Italian political parties in the Government of Understanding in Trieste. I even went to Rome as a member of a delegation to ask that the work for the rehabilitation of the power ship *Biancamano* be assigned to the shipyards in Trieste. I told various people about what I had done. I talked about it with De Gasperi, with Pella, with the President of the Liberals of Trieste, Forti.[7]

"I had kept a diary," Perlasca continues, "and I gave it to the newspaper, *Il Messaggero Veneto*. But they didn't do anything with it, so in 1952 I went and took it back. No, it seemed as if nobody was interested. I didn't hear from anyone in Budapest, and I had to figure out how to earn a living. And I'm not ashamed to recall that there were a lot of times when I had trouble putting together two square meals.

"And so it happened that, slowly but surely, I began to forget about it myself. I thought about it often, naturally, but I started to have my doubts. Was it true what happened to the Jews in Budapest? Were all the things I did in those few months really true? More than once I had my doubts. And I would stop myself and say, 'Giorgio, let's try and recollect the dates and the circumstances.' I sat down and thought about it, and everything came back: the dates, the places, the people. I wasn't wrong. It really did happen." What happened to Perlasca, the savior, was also what happened to the victims. As Primo Levi always recalled, the idea that they were not believed was common to many of those who had been prisoners in the concentration camps. In *The Drowned and the Saved* he wrote, "Almost all of the survivors, in written memoirs or oral conversations, recall a frequently recurring dream from their nights in prison, with some variation in the details but substantially the same dream. They are back home again talking with a dear friend or family member, recounting with passion and relief the pain that they had suffered, and they are not believed; even worse they're not even listened to. In its most typical (and cruelest) form, the listener would turn and silently walk away." Primo Levi did not succeed in publishing *Survival at Auschwitz* until thirteen years after the end of the war. The first book published in Italy to tell about the Nazi war crimes, *The Scourge of the Swastika* by Lord Edward Russell of Liverpool, had come out only three years earlier. Remembering was slow and difficult. When the war ended, for months and months, the Italian soldiers who had been deported to the Nazi camps after September 8 returned home. There were six hundred thousand of them, and they had been offered the chance to return home as free men if they would agree to wear the uniform of the Wehrmacht or the Republic of Salò.[8] Only an infamous few accepted the offer, but their stories were not told. They were considered "strange beasts" that the post-war couldn't figure out how to categorize, and their collective experience has still not found its place in the history books.

People did come to know, naturally, about the Italian Jews who were deported. But not quickly. And not everything. Italy was ready to absolve itself of responsibility for their fate, preferring instead to boast about the humane popular network that had provided so many of them with a hiding place and other assistance. The crimes were blamed on German domination. But, even today, few people know, for example, that the racial laws were not immediately abrogated upon the fall of fascism, as one might have expected. For reasons of prudence with regard to his German former allies, Marshal Pietro Badoglio waited seven months before canceling the most infamous of the discriminatory provisions. And, even today, few people know that the deportation of 8,566 Jews from Italy was carried out, unfortunately, with the active collaboration of the Italian bureaucracy and anonymous informers. Only now, thanks to a book called *Il libro della memoria* (The Book of Memory), a volume disturbing for its sheer size, its documentation, and its numbers, is it possible to read about what happened. The book was written by Liliana Piciotto Fargion, who dedicated ten years of her own life to finding survivors and anyone else in a position to provide information. The stories, the circumstances and the names, in alphabetical order, take up 538 pages. A few lines for each person on the list that begins with Abeasis Alberto, detained at Fossoli, deported from Verona, and liberated at Bergen Belsen, and ends with Vilma (surname unknown), who was detained first at the barracks in Fiume, then in the jail in Trieste, then deported to Auschwitz, and whose date and place of death are unknown. A work of documentation completed almost at the last possible moment. Only a few years more and the sources wouldn't have been alive anymore.

None of the Italians responsible for the deportation were punished. And, according to the unwritten law of compensation, there was silence for the saviors as well. That's what the wall was made of – the wall that Perlasca ran into when he returned home. A whole lot of denial and very little interest in making comparisons. If one man alone – modest, without any solid political connections – had succeeded in such an undertaking, why then had others not acted as he had? Then too, his story had taken place in Hungary, a long way from Italy and a country where, after the war, history was quickly silenced and memories smothered. The persecution of the Hungarian Jews is still a little known story. And yet it took place before the eyes of the world. The organized extermination campaign lasted eight months, from March 1944, to January 1945, when Hitler had already lost the war, in the middle of the simultaneous advance of the Red Army from the east and the Anglo-American forces from the west. It was a pre-announced extermination, foreseen and followed in all of its phases by diplomatic delegations and, day after day, in the international press. It was also the only holocaust to be interrupted by the abrupt retreat of the Nazi army, which meant that Budapest was the only central European city whose Jewish population was not completely exterminated. If tens of thousands were saved, we owe it to the rescue operation carried out by a small group of diplomats from the neutral countries who stayed on in the Hungarian capital through the final days of the siege.

Nothing about this whole story is very well known, except for one name, that of Raoul Wallenberg, the Swedish diplomat sent by the King of Sweden, with ample financial resources and the assignment to save the greatest number possible of Hungarian Jews. But even more than for the work he did, Wallenberg's name became famous because he disappeared at the time of the Soviet army's entrance into Budapest, and even today, after half a century, his fate is surrounded by a mystery that Moscow has still not completely cleared up. For two years now, however, we have known about another Wallenberg in the person of the Italian businessman, Giorgio Perlasca.

The two could not have been more different in their similarity; the one rich and protected, with a special status that allowed him to negotiate with the SS and offer money in exchange for human lives. The other, alone and on the run, paying for food on the black market out of his own pocket to ensure the survival of the people under his protection. The two met on various occasions during those months.

"At the freight station, for example," Perlasca recalls, "where we would go to try and pull anyone we could off the trains. Wallenberg was really good. He put his heart into it. I also ran into him at the Spanish diplomatic mission during the final days of the siege. On January 18, when the Russians had already entered the city, I had it on reliable information that Wallenberg was in a house in Király street. I went to see him, but they told me that he had gone out. I think that was the day he was killed, by a bomb or a stray bullet. After the war, when his case came up, I did the only thing I could. In 1952, I went to Milan and signed an affidavit about what I knew of the circumstances on the last day that I know for sure he was alive. . . . I thought they would call me, but I never heard anything more about it."

"Since he's been discovered," his wife says, "Giorgio has been rejuvenated."

"It would be better to say that my life has been turned upside down," says Giorgio. "But, sure, I was happy about it. There have been some really satisfying things that I'll never be able to forget. I hadn't gone back to Hungary since the end of the war. When they invited me for the award ceremony, I arrived in Budapest by train. We pulled into the station at Budapest, and I leaned out the window; I wanted to see if I could remember the old places. As the train pulled in, I could see a lot of people waiting on the platform, and I said to myself, I wonder what's going on? When I got off the train, I realized that they were waiting for me. They decorated me with the Order of the Gold Star, and I pinned it to the button hole of my jacket. That's the highest official honor that they give in Hungary. Just think, I would walk down the street or ride on a train, and people would stop and tip their hat to me. They would greet me and click their heels. Some people even gave me a military salute.

"Sometimes now I meet people who say they remember me. But, unfortunately, I can't remember them because they were children at the time. The ones I knew are all dead by now. I can see that they're disappointed when I can't remember them. But what can I do? They were children back then. And there were so many of them."

I've seen Giorgio Perlasca a number of times in the past two years. In addition to the Israeli and Hungarian decorations, he has received awards from Spain (oddly enough, the commendation of the Order of Isabella, the Catholic queen who ordered the expulsion of the Jews in 1492) and from the United States, at ceremonies in Washington and New York. ("By now, every time I leave, my grandson asks me, 'Grandpa, how many medals are you going to bring me this time?' "). In Italy, his story has been told on the television program "Mixer," and on that occasion I had the chance to accompany him to a private meeting with the President of the Republic. We had arranged things very badly and parked the car in the wrong place, and so we had to walk a long way through the gardens of the presidential palace. Perlasca was partly amused and partly annoyed. "Nothing like this has ever happened to me. In Budapest and Jerusalem the car took me right up to the door."

Perlasca had a brief conversation with President Francesco Cossiga, who thanked him "as a man and as an Italian" for everything he had done. On his way out, Perlasca said that he had been afraid that they were going to offer him a Knight's Cross. "You know what Vittorio Emanuele used to say, don't you? No one should be denied a cigar and a Knight's Cross."[9]

But up to now they haven't offered it to him. Not the Knight's Cross or anything else either. And for Perlasca this is a disturbing oversight, as well as something he can't quite bring himself to understand.

Endnotes

1. On September 8, 1943, Italy signed an armistice with the Allied powers, breaking its alliance with Germany. Some six weeks earlier, on July 25, following a vote of no confidence by the Fascist Grand Council, Mussolini had been deposed and arrested. His successor, Marshal Pietro Badoglio, negotiated and signed the armistice with the Allies.

2. *Generale Della Rovere,* directed by Roberto Rossellini, and *La Grande Guerra* (The Great War), directed by Mario Monicelli, shared the Leone D'Oro award for the best film at the Venice film festival in 1959. In Rossellini's film, Vittorio De Sica plays a small-time con man who poses as a general in the Italian army and accepts bribes from the families of prisoners of war in return for his intervention on their behalf with the German authorities. Arrested and threatened with execution by the German police, he agrees to take on the identity of a partisan commander, General Della Rovere, in order to get information from his fellow prisoners about the resistance. Gradually his conscience gets the better of him, and he plays the role to the end, going to his death before a firing squad together with real partisan prisoners. In *La Grande Guerra* Sordi and Gassman, two of Italy's great comic actors, play two unsuccessful draft evaders, Oreste and Giovanni, who are captured by the Austrians as they are hiding out trying to avoid combat. Threatened with execution if they refuse to give information about their unit, they almost give in but then, when Giovanni (Gassman) is executed for insulting the arrogant Austrian officer who is interrogating them, Oreste follows his example and accepts death rather than talk.

3. Fiume is the Italian name for the Dalmatian city of Rijeka, now part of Croatia. Gabriele D'Annunzio (1863–1938) – poet, novelist, dramatist, soldier and politician – dominated the Italian literary scene at the turn of the century. His oratory had much to do with Italy's decision to fight in World War I, and in September 1919, embittered over Italy's poor treatment at the Versailles

treaty negotiations, he led a march on Fiume and occupied the city against the wishes and diplomatic commitments of the Italian government. The occupation lasted until December 1920, when the Treaty of Rapallo between Italy and Yugoslavia declared Fiume an independent city. One historian has called D'Annunzio's occupation of Fiume "the first of a series of subversive acts from the right that was to culminate in Mussolini's march on Rome" in October 1922. (Giuliano Procacci, *History of the Italian People*, trans. Anthony Paul (Hammondsworth: Penguin Books, 1973).

4. Emilio Salgari (1862–1911), the author of dozens of popular adventure tales about pirates, sea captains and valiant soldiers of fortune conquering romantic foreign lands.

5. On October 3, 1935, Mussolini launched an invasion of Ethiopia, starting a war that would end seven months later in an Italian victory and the establishment of the Empire of Italian East Africa, whose crown was to be worn by King Vittorio Emanuele III. Perlasca's brigade, "the October 28th," took its name from October 28, 1922, the date that Vittorio Emanuele, in the face of the threatened Fascist march on Rome, refused to sign a declaration of martial law and instead invited Mussolini to take control of the government.

6. *Il manifesto degli scienziati razzisti* (The Manifesto of the Racial Scientists) was published anonymously on July 14, 1938, in the newspaper *Giornale d'Italia*. Not until July 25, 1938, were the names of its authors revealed, ten so-called "experts," at least four of whom were young university assistants vulnerable to political pressure, and only one of whom had national stature. See Susan Zuccotti, *The Italians and the Holocaust* (New York: Basic Books, 1987).

7. The *Fronte dell'Uomo Qualunque* (The Common Man's Front) was a movement that grew up around a magazine of the same name founded in December 1944, by Guglielmo Giannini. As its name implies, the party's rallying cry was a protest against political parties and professional politicians, but it attracted a

large number of followers from the ranks of ex-Fascists who were opposed to the anti-fascism of post-liberation Italy.

Alcide De Gasperi (1881–1954) was one of the founders of the Christian Democratic Party and Prime Minister in eight successive governments from 1945 to 1953. He championed close cooperation with the United States and Italy's membership in the NATO alliance.

Giuseppe Pella (1902–1981) served as a cabinet minister in several of De Gasperi's governments and was Prime Minister himself from August 1953, to January 1954, during which period Italy regained sovereignty over the city of Trieste. Pella was prominent in Italian politics up until 1972 when he last served as Minister of the Budget.

8. The Republic of Salò is the popular name of the *Repubblica Sociale Italiana*, based in the town of Salò on the western shore of Lake Garda, and which Mussolini established after his escape from prison in September 1943. As Paul Ginsborg has written, "Salò was chosen because it was felt that both the person and the authority of the Duce would have more chance of surviving there than in the great working-class cities of Milan and Turin. The government of Salò enjoyed nominal control over the whole of northern Italy, but the ageing and dispirited Mussolini was now little more than a useful figurehead for the Germans. It was they who gave the orders, and amongst the first of these was the rounding up and deportation to extermination camps of as many of the Italian Jews as they could find." P. Ginsborg, *A History of Contemporary Italy: Society and Politics 1943–1988* (London, 1990), p. 14.

9. The Knight's Cross was a medal representing membership in one of the five subdivisions of the Order of the Italian Crown instituted in 1868 by King Vittorio Emanuele II to celebrate the completion of the unification of Italy. When the monarchy was replaced by a parliamentary democracy after the Second World War, the Order of the Crown was renamed the Order of Merit of the Republic.

II
Memory Is a Woman

One day, sometime in 1987, Giorgio Perlasca found a letter in his mailbox from Germany informing him that he had been "discovered."

The following year, Perlasca learned exactly how he had been found. It wasn't that some institution or historian had remembered him. He had been tracked down by a group of women, who, now that they had located him, also wanted to help him. But above all, they wanted his name to be remembered.

"Operation Perlasca" was conceived in the living room of a house in Berlin, the home of Dr. Eveline Blitstein Willinger, an immunologist.

This is how she tells it:

"Twenty years ago, together with my family, I emigrated from Transylvania to Berlin where I began work as a researcher at the university. In a very short time, I came to know a lot of people of Hungarian origin, many of whom became very close friends. We fell into the habit of getting together once a month to talk about our past lives, books that we had read, our work. Four years ago, at one of these get-togethers, the discussion turned to the subject of prejudice and racial injustice and, from there, to Raoul Wallenberg, the King of Sweden's envoy to Budapest, who had disappeared mysteriously when the Red Army arrived in the city. It was already getting late, when one of the group, Mrs. Irene von Borosceny, asked to speak. Irene was a Hungarian countess, and when she was young she had worked for the International Red Cross in Budapest, during the closing months of the war. That night, as she talked, there was a touch of bitterness in her voice. She had known Wallenberg personally. But, she told us, she had also known another exceptional man, an Italian by the name of Giorgio Perlasca. A man who had given everything for the cause and who had been completely forgotten.

"I remember how silent the room became while Irene was talking. I had never heard that name before that night. The meeting broke up and, as we were leaving, Irene told us that she had kept some old documents and that she would tell us everything she knew about Perlasca at the next meeting.

"One week later we met again at the home of Dr. Vera Braun. There were just six of us, all women, and Irene von Borosceny talked for over two hours. Then it was our turn, and we all asked a bunch of questions. But by that time, I wasn't really completely present any more. Part of me had gone far away, back to the year 1944, to Budapest. I had returned to the splendid and familiar streets of Budapest at a time when Jews were not allowed to walk down them anymore. I saw desperate women holding on to their children, people waiting to be deported without any idea of their final destination. I saw young people confused and demoralized, unable to help their relatives. And, naturally, I saw there among them the dear faces of my grandparents, my uncles and aunts and my cousins. Faces that I know only from photographs. Then I could see the German 'Übermenschen' and the streets crowded with indifferent bystanders and passersby. . . . This is the scene that I always see when I close my eyes and think of my childhood and of my relatives who died at Auschwitz, Dachau and in Galicia, and of those who survived but were never able to free themselves of the scars left by the humiliation they had suffered in Budapest.

"As Irene spoke, I began to tremble. I remember that it was

very hard for me to fall asleep that night. I kept asking myself, how is it possible that a person like that is living somewhere in Italy and nobody has ever even heard his name? Why is it that the people he saved haven't told the world about him? Why haven't the newspapers written articles about him? Why hasn't the Italian government honored him as an exceptional person?

"So I decided to take the initiative and form a group to help Perlasca. My sister, Dr. Maria Vera Willinger, became the first member, and then we were joined by Dr. Maria Hedig, Professor Diamanstein, Dr. Ruth Gross, Attorney Heribert Hanish and Mrs. Anne Marie Brunner. We found out his address and decided to send him a monthly financial contribution. When I read Perlasca's diary (Irene got it for us; Perlasca had given it to Jenö Lévai, the historian of the Hungarian Holocaust), I was in total admiration of the man, and I decided that he must be one of the 'Thirty-Six Just Men.'

"It's a story from the Talmud that my father used to tell me when I was a child. At every moment in history there are always Thirty-Six Just Men in the world. They are born Just, and they can't abide injustice. It was because of His love for them that God did not destroy the world. Nobody knows who they are, and what's more, even they themselves don't know who they are. But they know how to recognize other people's suffering and take it on their shoulders. . . . I really liked that story as a young girl. It made me feel secure. When I grew up and learned that 6 million people had been killed because they prayed to God in a different way than their murderers, I asked my father what had happened to the Thirty-Six Just Men during that time. Why didn't they appear and lend a hand?

"When Perlasca came into my life, I thought again about the legend of the Just Men and I got the idea to write to Yad Vashem – the museum-archive of the Holocaust in Jerusalem – to ask that they recognize him as one of the Just. I sent the letters and documents that Irene had given us. They replied that in order to name Perlasca as one of the Just, it would be necessary to find witnesses and conduct an investigation. That was when Vera Braun came up with the idea that turned out to be decisive: to publish a notice in the newspapers in Jerusalem and Budapest."

The notice appeared in "Uj Elet" (*New Life*), a Jewish periodical published in Budapest, on May 15, 1988.

> We are looking for anyone who, in 1944–45, had occasion to know Giorgio (Jorge) Perlasca, a man of Italian origin who was at that time employed at the Spanish embassy and who, it seems, had a role in the organization of the Spanish safe houses. Anyone who knows anything about the activities of the above-mentioned person is hereby requested to contact the Director of the National Rabbinical Institute, Rabbi Dr. József Schweiber.

"Immediately after the publication of the notice," Dr. Blitstein Willinger recalls, "something happened that, to me, is really extraordinary. There were still people alive who remembered. They contacted the Rabbi, brought in their certificates of protection and recounted the events, places and circumstances in which they had met him. They were happy to testify about everything Perlasca had done for them. All the material was sent to Yad Vashem. A short time later, the answer came back from Jerusalem: the Commission for the Designation of the Just had decided to confer on Signor Perlasca, as a sign of its highest recognition, a gold medal and the right to plant a tree on the Street of the Just on Mount Remembrance in Jerusalem.

"Perlasca had to postpone his visit to Israel for almost a year for health reasons. But he was able to get there on September 24, 1989. And before that he went to Budapest, where a special session of the Parliament awarded him the Gold Star of Hungary. He wrote to tell me that in Budapest he had stayed in the Hotel Astoria, the same place where he had lived forty years earlier, that he had met many kind people, and that he was very satisfied with the visit."

"Satisfied and moved," says Perlasca, "when I learned how

my name had come out. Contessa von Borosceny? Certainly I remember her. She was very young at the time, and we were friends. She did some really important things back then. She passed me a lot of useful information and made sure messages got through. She knew I wasn't a diplomat, but she was one of the people who helped me the most, especially with moral support. It was truly moving to learn that she was the one who had remembered me."

In September 1988, among the millions of tourists crowding onto the beaches in Rimini (on Italy's Adriatic Coast), there were two people who couldn't have cared less about the place, an elderly couple from Budapest who had come on one of the many organized tours. They were very thin and their skin was almost bleach-white. They didn't go to the beach. They didn't go shopping. They didn't go to the restaurants.

Mr. and Mrs. Lang, Eva and Pál, had chosen the "all-inclusive tour" offered by the Health Workers Union, for one reason only. Besides Rimini, the vacation package included excursion trips to Rome, Florence, Ravenna and Venice. But what interested them most about the itinerary was a free afternoon in Padua, on the way back home.

In 1988, freedom of movement for Hungarian tourists was not as easy as it is today. It was Eva who had discovered the possibility of the trip to Italy and who had made sure that her and her husband's names were on the list way ahead of time. They calculated the hours that they would have available in Padua and wrote a letter to Signor Giorgio Perlasca announcing that they would be at his house on September 4 at three o'clock in the afternoon. Then Eva convinced her husband, at the age of 68, to dedicate himself completely to the study of Italian so that they would be able to conduct at least a minimal conversation with Signor Perlasca.

When the departure date finally came, Eva put together a suitcase full of gifts that would "remind Perlasca of the flavors of

Hungary." Inside, she put two different kinds of Magyar salami, a jar of ground paprika, a bottle of Tokay and one of Vinum Vitae, a box of rum-flavored macaroons of the sweet variety and a canned ham. In another envelope, Eva put two photographs of herself when she was young, a copy of the issue of the newspaper "Uj Elet" that carried her account of Perlasca's deeds, and several poems which she had dedicated to him. Then the original of the Spanish safe-conduct letter that had enabled her to save herself. Finally, some other presents, photographs of Budapest, a table cloth and some embroidered doilies.

In 1944, Miss Eva Konigsberg was twenty years old. She had married Mr. Pál Lang for the most material of motives. The German SS, which had been in Hungary since March, had set itself a single immutable objective: to find one hundred thousand Jews to be assigned to forced labor in service to the Reich. One of the many decrees issued by the Hungarian government in those months declared that "Husbands who leave for obligatory work assignments exempt their wives from the same obligation."

They were married in October in the City Hall and, on that same day, some five hundred weddings were celebrated, "partly true and partly false." Pál Lang was shipped off together with Eva's brother. Of the thousands and thousands who left in those days, walking through the streets of Budapest, forced into line by the SS, many died, killed for some minor violation of the rules or by the cold or starvation. Pál Lang ended up working, and being treated like a slave, in a stone quarry. From there, in the last weeks of the war, he was transferred to the concentration camp at Mauthausen.

Eva remained in Budapest. She and her father, a veteran of the First World War who had spent five years in prison in Vladivostok, were ordered to clean the streets of the city of the debris created by the American bombing. They were among the few Jews who were allowed outside wearing the yellow star that all Jews in the capital had been forced to put on their clothes. Eva Lang wore a pair of work overalls with a yellow star sewn on the front.

The order to wear the yellow star at all times was issued on April 5, 1944. It said, "All Jews over six years of age must wear a star, ten by ten centimeters, color canary yellow, made of cloth, silk or velvet, sewn tightly on the left front of their clothing or overcoat. War heroes and the seriously disabled shall be exempt." A few days later, another decree exempted the wives, widows and children of war heroes or soldiers killed in action, converted Jews married to Christians, and pastors and deacons of Jewish origin.

Eva was a very pretty girl, with blue eyes as big as lakes. She had a privilege over the others, a "pass" that allowed her to go out on the streets, but she knew that every chance meeting could be dangerous. As soon as the decrees were issued, in fact, it was open season in the hunt for Jews on the streets of Budapest. A lot of people were beaten up or arrested by bands of Nazis or police squads who claimed that their stars were not the right shade of yellow or didn't measure up to the required dimensions. They would stick a pen in between two stitches and if the pen passed through they would say that the star hadn't been sewn on correctly. And it was always possible to force the pen through the gap.

On April 20, a new decree established that the star had to be worn on both sides. On April 27, that the star was not to be covered by scarves or any other object such as suitcases or musical instruments. The Jewish Council recommended that everyone follow orders and collaborate. And they weren't alone. "Radio Kossuth,"[1] which broadcast from Moscow and carried news of the advance of the Soviet troops, encouraged the Jews to wear the yellow star and to "wear it with pride." Then, one day in June, the Konigsbergs' house was searched, and the radio was not to be heard anymore. It was confiscated, along with their skis and Eva's brother Gyögy's fencing foil.

On November 12, 1944, Eva Lang née Konigsberg decided to try to corrupt a policeman. In exchange for some money she got him to give her a one-day exemption from the forced labor. She had heard that the Spanish delegation was giving out letters of protection. She had also heard that the certificates were issued to anyone who asked, and that it wasn't necessary to pay. Hidden in one of her inside pockets that morning, Eva carried a number of photographs: hers; one of her husband, Pál; one of her brother, Gyögy; and one each of her mother, her father and her two cousins.

She ran as fast as she could to the embassy headquarters, in Eötvös Street, where she was stopped by a huge line outside on the sidewalk. She finally made her way to the entrance and handed over the photographs. They were assigned numbers 200 and 201. That's where she saw Perlasca for the first time. She didn't know who that man was, but he was certainly a foreigner. He didn't speak Hungarian.

Leaving the embassy, she was happy. In the pocket of her overalls she was carrying two letters of protection, written in Hungarian and German. The family photographs had been attached to the letters, which were just a few lines long:

> Relatives resident in Spain have requested Spanish citizenship for these persons. The Spanish legation is authorized to grant them a travel visa. The Spanish legation requests that the competent authorities take this matter into consideration in the application of any measures and that the above-named persons be exempted from forced labor.

At dawn on November 13, Hungarian soldiers appeared at the front door of the building where the Konigsbergs were living and dragged all of the Jews outside. Eva looked up to see the faces of the Christians in the windows as they applauded the raid, but then, when the Jews were carried away by force, she saw them close their curtains in shame. Jews who converted to Catholicism enjoyed a few extra privileges. But they weren't easy to obtain. Eva knew a lot of people who had gone to the neighborhood parish to beg for them. But often they found themselves confronted by priests who started into long speeches. They wanted to be sure that the conversion was the result of serious contemplation. They refused to backdate certificates, saying that they didn't want to violate the law. They asked all kinds of finicky questions about doctrinal quesions like the virginity of the Blessed Mother or asked people to recite the Our Father by heart.

The Jews from her building were taken to a camp to wait to be deported. Eva's mother was able to hand some stranger a message with their names written on it. "Take this immediately to the Spanish legation." The man did as she said, but it took him a day and a half to get through the line outside the embassy. In the end, however, he made it inside and delivered the message. Later, a man whom Eva doesn't remember very well, but who was probably Perlasca, arrived at the camp and read their names out through a megaphone. They raised their hands. "These people are under the protection of the Spanish government!" he said, with a very self-assured tone. The soldiers let them go. Eva and her family were thus able, at least for the moment, to escape deportation.

Two days later, on November 18, Eva Lang went out to the street again. This time she had with her, in her overalls, a wad of money that her family had entrusted to her.

She walked up to a soldier and asked, "Do you want to make some money?" He answered yes, and Eva gave him some very precise directions. "Here are 1,000 pengö.[2] Go to the camp." She gave him the name of a doctor relative of theirs who they knew was still there. "Bring him to our house and then escort all of us to the Spanish safe house at 35 St. Stephen's Park. When we get there, there'll be another 3,000 pengö for you."

The soldier did it. Not only that, but besides the doctor relative, he brought along somebody else whom the Langs didn't even know. Accompanied by the soldier, they all went to the house in St. Stephen's Square.

The building was six stories high, and the Spanish flag was

flying above the front door. Below the house, the banks of the Danube. In the middle of the river Margarita Island, and on the other side, the hills of Buda. The Langs lived in that building for three months, together with a thousand other people.

Eva was set up on the sixth floor, under the roof terrace. There were sixty-five people in two rooms. At the end of November the temperature dropped suddenly, and the thermometer went below zero. The water pipes burst, and they resorted to drinking melted snow. The Danube began to freeze into big blocks of ice. The banks were covered with snow. The snow turned red when the Jews were taken down to the river to be killed.

Right under that building, day after day, thousands of people were pushed and shoved down to the river. Some tried to escape toward the diplomatic refuge and were killed. All of them begged and screamed as they were dragged down to the banks. The killing was done at the edge of the river. The victims were ordered to take off their shoes. Then, in pairs, they were tied together with wire. Only one of the two would be shot with a bullet to the head and, falling into the river, would pull the other in with him. And the pair would then die together, in the ice cold waters of the Danube.

At the end of November, Eva Lang got the news that her husband and brother had been deported but that they were still alive. The booming sounds of Stalin's artillery batteries began to roll down on the city from the hills of Buda while, below the building, bands of Nyilas – as the young pro-Nazi militants were called – tried continually to capture people living in the house and take them away to be killed.

In the two rooms on the sixth floor it was decided that each person had the right to one meter of space. In that space you could argue, you could shout out loud, and you could pray. There was no sense of community because there was nothing to share. In December, food began to grow short. The Jewish Council sent some tea and some beans.

Quite often, Eva Lang would escape from her space and go

out onto the terrace. She met a boy out there who was so agile that he could jump from one roof to another and visit all of the houses in St. Stephen's Park. Somehow or other this boy had got his hands on a pair of binoculars, and he and Eva would train them on the hills of Buda and follow the progress of the battle. The boy would jump around the rooftops every day. He would come back with things he had found and something to eat. One day he came back with a little girl he had found hiding behind a chimney.

(Like Eva, the "jumping boy" survived the war. He became an adult and then an old man. When the notice about Perlasca was published in the newspaper, Eva Lang called him and asked him to testify. But he didn't do it. And he wasn't alone. Eva Lang came to understand that not everybody was glad, after all that time, to talk about those months. And she also understood that not everybody was happy to recognize that someone else had saved their lives.)

One day in December 1944, Eva Lang burned her hands on a pan. They were bandaged, and with her bandaged hands she went to stand in line for food. She was given a can of sardines that she carried away. But the can slipped out of her hands on the stairs. The can was round and the stairs circled downward inside a spiral staircase. The can kept on rolling down the steps and Eva ran after it. She ended up two floors down. And there she saw a man – "tall and blond" – confronting a group of Nyilas who were trying to come up the stairs. She heard them yelling, and she saw them grab him. The tall blond man pushed them back off the stairs. He shouted that they did not have permission to go up-stairs, that the entire building was under the protection of the Spanish government, that they were on Spanish territory. It was the same man whom she had seen at the Spanish legation.

Eva succeeded in getting her can of sardines and ran back up-stairs. But she saw that man again. He came to bring food and to order everyone not to leave the building, not for any reason whatsoever.

There was a lot of talk about that man in St. Stephen's Park, but nobody knew who he was. Eva and the other girls thought he was good looking. A handsome gentleman, with an elegant suit. A hero. His name, Perlasca, was pronounced after the Hungarian fashion, with the accent on the first syllable: Pérlasca. Or better yet, with that little bit of aspiration and suspension that Hungarians typically put in the middle of the word, "Pér—Lasca." So a lot of people came to believe that the Spanish gentleman was really named Lasca and that the "Pér" in front of his name was some kind of noble title, like the English "Sir." In the building, people said that he was an important ambassador, that he had been sent by the Americans, and that the fate of the world depended on him.

The bus carrying the travelers from the Health Workers Union dropped off its passengers in Padua around noon. Pál Lang walked up to a taxi and asked the driver, in his uncertain Italian, to take them to Via Guglielmo Marconi, behind the Prato della Valle. For some reason, both he and his wife had got the idea that the place was a long way from the center of town. But the taxi ride was over in less than ten minutes.

So Eva and Pál Lang got to Perlasca's house two hours early. They sat down on a bench and waited; they didn't ring the doorbell until three o'clock sharp.

They talked for the whole time until they had to go back to the bus. Pál's Italian, though still rudimentary, proved to be useful. But Perlasca remembered a little Hungarian, and they filled in the gaps with German. "He was very happy with the gifts," Eva recalls. "He smiled when he saw the safe conduct letter. I wished he could remember me . . . that incident on the stairs. But he didn't give me that satisfaction. He told me that he just couldn't remember. But he was sorry."

Endnotes

1. Lajos Kossuth (1802–1894), Hungarian revolutionary leader who tried to win Hungary's independence from Austria in 1848. He briefly led a provisional revolutionary government in 1849 until Russian troops intervened to restore Austrian authority.

2. Hungarian currency from the period between the two wars (a popular song went, "If I had 200 pengö a month I'd be doing fine . . ."). During the war, due to inflation, it was devalued several times.

III
"Hungaria Felix"

When the war broke out, Signor Giorgio Perlasca was thirty years old and had already fought in two wars. He wasn't going to wear any more uniforms. He married a girl from Trieste, Nerina Dal Pin, and found himself a job. He worked for a company called SAIB – Società Anonima Importazione Bovini (Livestock Import Company) – and his assignment was to negotiate the purchase of livestock on the Balkan peninsula and arrange for transport to Italy in cattle cars. The SAIB had a monopoly on the importation of meat. In addition to money, purchases could be paid for "in-kind": livestock in exchange for cloth, hats, or socks. The imported livestock was slaughtered in Italy and turned into canned meat or rations for the armed forces, and particularly for sailors on submarines.

Perlasca didn't fight in the war, but he soon became caught up in it. He was in Yugoslavia when the Germans came down from the north to occupy it.

Today, when he's asked what people in Budapest knew about what was happening to the Jews, he jumps to answer, "Everybody knew! . . . Everybody knew what was happening to the Jews under Hitler. The diplomats knew, and their governments knew." Then he looks you in the eye: "If I knew, and I was just a simple businessman, all those people who were better informed than I was had to know, don't you think?"

And just what did you know? "I knew what I saw with my own eyes. It was impossible not to know."

And what did you see? "I was there when the Jews were being deported from Belgrade. It was 1941. My wife was there with me too. One morning, a line of carriages, escorted by the SS and crammed full of Jewish women from the city, passed right under our window. They were singing a religious hymn. I can still hear the sound of their voices. I remember those women very well; they were fully aware that they were going toward a dark destiny, but they were also very proud. The hymn they were singing was not a song of desperation. And yet they knew full well that they were being taken away.

"It was impossible not to understand what was happening. I was living in the home of a dentist, a Dr. Grin. They took him away too, with his family. If I had only known about it ahead of time, I think I could have got them permission to come to Italy. But by the time I realized it, it was too late. They took the gypsies away too. My wife and I used to go to a restaurant where a gypsy band played music. Then one night they weren't there anymore. We asked what had happened to them, and the owner said, 'They were rounded up and taken away with the rest of the gypsies.'"

At the end of 1942, pushed by the war farther and farther away from home, Perlasca arrived in Hungary. "Budapest was different. It seemed untouched by the war. There was plenty of food, and you could still work and earn a living; the city's famous night life went on as if nothing had changed. And for Italians, being in Budapest was a little like being home. Sure, there was some anti-Semitism there too, but compared to what I had seen in Yugoslavia, I can assure you it was like rose water."

Cosmopolitan Budapest, the second pearl of the Hapsburg Empire, Vienna's little sister. For today's tourists it's an unknown wonder, waiting to be discovered, but fifty years ago, for Italians, Budapest was the fascinating capital of a friendly nation.

Or, more accurately, just like Vienna, it was an enemy in World War I but became a friend just four years later.

By a quirk of history unthought of and unforseen by the political strategists of the time, when the Hapsburg Empire collapsed, Hungary, unlike every other European country, experienced what had been predicted and feared ever since Lenin had come to power in Russia: a victorious "Bolshevik insurrection." The whole thing lasted just one hundred and thirty-three days, from the day Béla Kun (a Communist educated in the Soviet Union, where he had been a prisoner of war) overthrew, almost without a fight, the liberal-socialist government of Count Karoly and proclaimed a "Republic of the Councils."

Everything was nationalized and sovietized. Government decrees ordered huge salary increases, reductions in rent and a shorter work week. The nobles fled the city, seeking refuge in Vienna and Szeged, in the south of Hungary, while Budapest threw itself passionately into its brief Communist interlude. It was a fierce utopia, brought to an end by an offensive of the Romanian army, which forced the capital to its knees and Béla Kun to surrender. The nobles' counter-attack began in Szeged, led by Count Miklós Horthy, Admiral of the Austro-Hungarian Imperial Navy. His troops reclaimed the capital and, while Béla Kun and the members of the government of the "Republic of the Councils" fled to Vienna, installed the new government.

Horthy, an admiral in a country which no longer had a navy nor an opening to the sea, named himself regent of the Crown of Hungary in the name of Charles of Hapsburg, the non-existent ruler of an Empire that had been dissolved. He unleashed the "white terror" against the socialists and the Jews (accused of having been enthusiastic supporters of the Republic led by the Jew Béla Kun) just as Béla Kun, during his 133 days in power, had unleashed the "red terror" against the nobles, the land owners and the church. The first regime carried out 585 executions; the restoration responded with 1,500. Hungary became the first European country that had victoriously opposed the Bolshevik threat.

But more than the Bolshevik interlude, the real wound that left its mark on Hungary was the Treaty of Trianon of June, 1920. As part of the Danubian monarchy, Hungary was held responsible for the war and was forced to cede Slovakia to Czechoslovakia, Croatia and Slovenia to Yugoslavia, Banat to Yugoslavia and Romania, and Transylvania to Romania. Altogether, Hungary lost two-thirds of its territory and two-thirds of its previous population, 14 million people. In addition, the winning powers allowed the new "Little Hungary" to maintain an army of no more than 35,000 men. The reconquest of the territories lost in the "unjust peace" and the search for allies able to help in the battle thus became the dominant themes of the country's politics until the end of the Second World War.

For much of that time, Mussolini's Italy was one of the most sought-after potential allies. During the 1930s and '40s, Hungary and Italy developed an intense political, commercial and cultural relationship.

During that twenty-year period, Hungary looked rather like the absurd translated into reality. An endless hierarchy of nobles owned two-thirds of the land. A military caste, clad in stupendous uniforms, kept up its chivalrous rituals, while boasting not a single victory. The public administration and bureaucracy continued to be just as precise, punctilious and fair as it had been under Franz Joseph. The country was deeply Catholic, but the state allowed divorce. Vast plains supplied the country with meat, horses, geese and oil while in the countryside, and in the poorer neighborhoods of the capital, tuberculosis spread like wildfire.

And then there was Budapest, the city that outlived defeats, revolutions and restorations. Dedicated to commerce and to feeding the fantasies of Europeans, it lined up its docks along the Danube and its cafés along its wide boulevards. It transported goods along the river and welcomed passengers at its two railway stations, one on the east side of the city, and one on the west. It produced light opera, violins, newspapers, theater and cinema. In its restaurants, aging countesses lunched with their handsome younger lovers. As happens to only a few of the world's cities, Budapest fell in love with itself and its inhabitants, inviting them to enjoy its theatrical backdrop, feed on their stereotyped self-image, and refuse to accept the end of an era.

Even after World War II, Hollywood brought the city's personalities to the screen, polished to a shine like classic automobiles. In *The Prince and the Showgirl*, released in 1957, Laurence Olivier plays the role of the Carpathian Regent, sporting a monocle and a uniform that looks more like a plaster cast. Marilyn Monroe is the cute American girl who suddenly finds herself surrounded by royal intrigue. She calls him "Your Regency" and invites him – he is horrified – to hold free elections ("Do it, Your Regency. Elections are a real ball. You never know who's going to win!").

Mussolini took a liking to Admiral Horthy: a massive nobleman, loaded with medals, who had crossed the frozen Danube riding a white horse and who spoke Italian mixed with the Venetian dialect that he had learned aboard the Hapsburgs' ships. With Admiral Horthy in power, Italian fascism suddenly discovered that it had many and diverse ties to Hungary; it seemed almost like the joyful reunion of two long lost brothers. Italy's Risorgimento was compared to Hungary's 1848 revolution, led by Kossuth; the countries shared a common religious tradition going back to the Middle Ages; there had been artistic exchanges during the Renaissance. Italy offered the Hungarians the magnificent Palazzo Falconieri to use as their embassy in Rome. Horthy returned the favor by turning over the former seat of the Parliament, designed by the famous architect Miklós Ybl, to be used as the headquarters of the Italian Cultural Institute and by naming one of the city's central squares after Mussolini. Agreements on trade and customs exemptions were signed in Budapest and Rome, Fiume once again became a common Magyar-Italian port, and Italy was inundated with books on Hungarian pedagogy. Even more than in other parts of the world, Italian children came to know Budapest by reading *The*

Paul Street Boys, by Ferenc Molnár, the tender children's story about loyalty and pulmonary disease, friendship, homemade uniforms and banners flying around a badly kept field that was just good enough for a soccer game among the tenements of Pest.

Ferenc Molnár was a typical product of Hungary in those days. The son of a Jewish doctor from Budapest, he knocked on a newspaper editor's door one day, and his story was published in the next Sunday's paper. The story was very successful, and he decided to become a writer. He had a mad, passionate love affair with a star of the Hungarian theater. He loved Italy, one of his wives was Italian, and he was often seen at the Lido in Venice: a handsome man, dressed in white linen, with a monocle and a handkerchief in his breast pocket, and not the least bit bashful about telling Italian journalists of his admiration for Mussolini.

In the (seldom studied) Hungarian history of the twenty years between the two wars, the regime of Admiral Horthy is known as "Horthy's fascist regime." In reality, however, Hungarian politics were very complex. The parliamentary system survived through the first half of 1944, and elections, though not with universal suffrage, continued to be held. The lower house of Parliament included, among the others, representatives of the Socialist Party. Unions represented industrial workers. In 1926, a "Chamber of Nobles" or "Magnates" was instituted, along the lines of England's House of Lords, with representatives from the historic nobility and the professions, the public administration, and the churches – the Catholic Church of course, but also the Lutheran, and two representatives of the Jewish faith.

If the recovery of the lost territories continued to be the leading issue in Hungarian politics, second place was occupied by the "Jewish question." In Hungary the "Jewish question" was discussed on an almost daily basis in very material, and quite paradoxical, terms. Freed by the Hapsburgs over a hundred years before, the Jews, 5 percent of the country's total population, enjoyed the same rights as other citizens and were the "driving force" of the Hungarian economy. Budapest – or rather, its right half, Pest – was a truly Jewish city, even more compact than Warsaw. In a society weighed down by a long- and not-so-long-established nobility, absentee landowners and a military frustrated by defeat, the Jews represented the rising bourgeoisie. In Budapest, their presence was felt in the newspapers, the professions, banks, commerce, international trade and cultural exchange, and in all kinds of initiatives involving the most modern sectors of society, from the press and the theater to medicine and the cinema. In the 1930s, the Jewish population of Budapest was estimated at 20 percent, and it was quite a common experience to walk through neighborhoods with signs written in Hebrew, dozens of synagogues and schools, and daily papers and magazines that advertised themselves as Jewish publications.

Present in Hungary for almost a thousand years, many having come from Spain after the expulsion ordered by the Catholic monarchs in 1492, freed by the Hapsburgs in 1867 from the bonds that had rendered them citizens without rights, the Hungarian Jews, at least in the capital, were completely "assimilated." Mixed marriages were more and more numerous, Jewish families commonly celebrated Christmas, and not a few of them had added a noble title to the family name. Fully integrated into the Hungarian military, ten thousand of them had given up their lives in the First World War and, apart from the official Hungary of medals and ceremonies, it was quite evident to everyone that the national economy was dependent on the presence of the Jews.

In the capital, on the Danube, beyond Margarita Island, rose Csepel, the headquarters of the country's most important industry, the steelworks of Manfred Weiss. In the countryside, the social rise of Jewish immigrants had been rapid indeed. Having come from Galicia and entered into service with the nobility as "the house Jew" (the bookkeeper who kept the accounts for the carefree nobility), the Jews had obtained, in exchange for their services, larger and larger quantities of land, which they were able to make much more profitable than their employers. Dohány Street, in Pest, was the site of the largest temple in Europe. Dozens of synagogues were present throughout the city's neighborhoods. The MTK soccer team was the Jewish team, just like Honvéd was the army team and Ujpest was the police officers' team. For the inhabitants of Pest the Jews had always been "part of the landscape." They were Hungarians just like the Catholics – even if their holy day was Saturday and they didn't eat pork – but, they were more adept in commerce and more given to study. The unbearable objects of envy as the perennial first in their class, they were the consistent winners in the competition for jobs in the civil service.

What Giorgio Perlasca saw when he arrived in Budapest was in reality the veiled image of a looming catastrophe. The last remaining European capital whose synagogues could still be freely attended, a refuge city for Jews who had been able to escape ahead of the advancing Reich, in Budapest it was possible to see at the same time old Jews with the "kippa" sitting at the cafés, reading the newspapers and chatting in Yiddish, absolutely convinced that they were in what would always be their city, and militant bands of the pro-Nazi "Arrow Cross" Party, marching the streets and announcing the upcoming "definitive solution of the Jewish question."

But it was all happening openly; an endemic "social conflict" that had been developing in Hungary for the last twenty years and which was now growing more virulent. And yet it was still a Hungarian question, to be resolved in Hungary.

If in Poland peasants drank in anti-Semitism with mother's milk, if in Germany it had been instilled by the aggressivity of the Nazi Party, if in Italy it had arrived in one blow by virtue of an arbitrary decision made by Mussolini, in Hungary it had always been a nagging problem. The nobility, all of whom, following Horthy's lead, declared themselves "anti-Semitic," admitted openly that without the Jews the country would have immediately gone down the tubes. Each of a series of nobles who had been named head of the government relied on the Jews' knowledge and business expertise for the country's economic policy and efforts to attract foreign capital. The restrictions to be imposed on the Jews thus became a problem of choosing the right dosage, election campaign rhetoric, a propaganda theme.

Young people were a particularly receptive audience. After the collapse of the empire, the capital began to fill up with throngs of unemployed youth who had completed their education only to find that their career prospects were rather less than bright. The cause of their unemployment? The Jews, naturally.

It wasn't long before, in and around the boulevard cafés, a new association, "The Political Association of Unemployed Graduates," began to compile and disseminate the results of its detailed statistical studies. In Budapest, 60 percent of the doctors were Jewish; 53 percent of store owners; 50 percent of lawyers, 37 percent of managers in the mining industry (the most important industry in the country), and 70 percent of journalists. The "Unemployed Graduates" asked for legislation to protect them by imposing a quota on Jews in the professions.

In the meantime, while waiting for a secure job and bored with the world, the young denizens of Budapest spent their lives hanging out in the city's five hundred cafés. It was a good way to pass the time, but the café life also produced one of Europe's biggest best sellers in the 1930s, Ferenc Kormendi's *Adventure in Budapest*, a literary dissection of neurotic and small-minded ambition. And one of the café life's main players, László Josef Biró, also realized the dream of providing humanity with a revolutionary pen. While wandering around from one café to another, cooking up the most harebrained schemes, Biró managed to turn the aristocratic quill pen into the democratic ballpoint. Still others among the young unemployed, those who had the necessary energy, headed for Trieste and from there took to the sea.

It was the great escape, the American dream. Just as in Italy, at the beginning of the century emigration was massive – half a million people. And it continued into the 1920s and '30s. People fantasized about the new world where all men were equal and about American cities like Cleveland that had become new Hungarian centers. The newspapers carried the fairy story of the Hungarian József Pulitzer, who had emigrated to America at age sixteen without a penny and had gone on to become the country's most important newspaper publisher. And there was the story of Adolph Zukor (Cukor), the nephew of the Rabbi of Ricse, the home of Tokay wine, who emigrated to become the king of Hollywood.

It was said that anybody who left for Hollywood had a chance to become a movie star. One of those who left was a certain Béla Blaskó, who became famous as Bela Lugosi, or Dracula. America and the movies were part of everybody's dreams, so much so in fact that at the Zukor Studios they hung out a sign for new arrivals that said, "It's great you're Hungarian. But if you want a job, you better know how to do something too."

But the 1930s also brought from the United States the stock market crash and the Great Depression, followed rapidly by the imposition of immigration quotas. Now it was almost impossible to be welcomed as an immigrant and more difficult than ever to find a job at home. In Hungary, the military and the petty nobility started getting agitated. A nearby government was now headed by an Austrian corporal who said that it was all the fault of the Jews. His book, *Mein Kampf,* was a best seller in Budapest, just like in the rest of Europe. An obscure captain by the name of Gyula Gömbös emerged from the governmental establishment and founded the "Party for the Defense of the Race," whose primary objective was the expropriation of all property owned by Jews. He began to have a following. New athletic clubs and cultural organizations, in addition to the "Unemployed Graduates," began to spring up, calling for the expulsion of Jews from public employment, the confiscation of their land, and a fight against "soulless capitalism."

Very quickly, all of Europe was revealed to be ready to listen to the ideas of the Austrian corporal who had taken power in Berlin: the Jews are corruption and they rule the world; Europe must resolve the "Jewish question." Captain Gömbös boasted about the Nazis' achievements. In Germany they did things the right way; they attacked. There they got rid of the Jews all right, but before doing that, they made them give up all of their riches. And that's what Hungary should do too. It was the triumph of anti-Semitic statistics. Detailed studies provided daily information on how many square feet were occupied by the Jews, how many acres of land they owned, which properties they had acquired.

But alarm did not spread among the Hungarian Jews. And yet Zionism had originated with the idea of a journalist from Budapest, Theodor Herzl. At the end of the last century, in Paris, he had covered the trial of Captain Dreyfus and had been struck by the widespread anti-Semitism of French society. He concluded that the Jews would have to found a homeland of their own, and he imagined it being first in Argentina, then in Uganda, and finally in Palestine, in the sparsely populated lands of the Bible. He had some followers in Budapest. But in Hungary, as in the rest of Europe, his was a minority position. For the 10 million Jews who lived in Europe, from Poland to Hungary, Czechoslovakia and Austria, from Greece to Yugoslavia, Italy, France and Holland, their respective countries of residence were their homelands; they didn't need a new one. Adolf Hitler's frenetic raving would soon be over.

In 1938, after the Nazi *Anschluss* of Austria on the eve of the war, the situation for the European Jews had become dangerous, and those who could, fled. The situation was so apparent that President Roosevelt called an international conference held in Evian, France, whose agenda included "The absorption of European Jews with the status of political refugees." The conference was attended by representatives from thirty-two countries, each of whom presented a plan for "reabsorption" that never saw the light of day. In 1979, as reported by *The New York Times*, Vice-President Walter Mondale talked about the Evian meeting during his speech in Geneva at the United Nations Conference on Indochinese Refugees:

> At Evian they began with high hopes. But they failed the test of civilization. The civilized world hid in a cloak of legalisms. Two nations said that they had reached the saturation point for Jewish refugees. Four nations said they would accept experienced agricultural workers only. One would only accept immigrants who had been baptized. Three declared intellectuals and merchants to be undesirable new citizens. One nation feared that the influx of Jews would arouse anti-Semitic feelings. And one delegate said this: 'As we have no real racial problem, we are not desirous of importing one.'[1]

The first Nazi-inspired, anti-Semitic legislation after the German laws of 1935 was approved in Hungary, in 1938, under pressure from the extreme right. The new laws established "quotas" in various professions for "Hungarian citizens of the Israelite faith." In the Chamber of Nobles the representatives of the churches accepted them as "the lesser evil" compared to what might have happened.

The next year, a second anti-Jewish law was introduced in the Hungarian Parliament. Besides imposing quotas for the exercise of certain professions, it contained language defining Jews as persons having one Jewish parent or two Jewish grandparents. The Parliamentary debate went on for months, and it was a unique event in all of Europe. In the history of anti-Semitic legislation, in fact, Hungary is the only country in which such laws were adopted not by an imperial or dictatorial act, but as a result of a parliamentary process that lasted years and which featured – in a sort of theatrical production staged on the edge of the abyss –

proponents and opponents, compromises, ingenuous enthusiasts and pessimistic Cassandras who, obviously, were not heeded.

Although the first set of anti-Semitic laws failed to give rise to much consternation or fear, during the debate over the second set the three largest Jewish organizations published the following appeal in the Budapest newspapers:

> Is this what Hungarian Jews deserve? The mutilation of our civil rights, the limitation of our private law, restrictions on our way of life, ostracism for our young people? Is this what the community of Hungarian Jews deserves when, in the course of over a century of history, their only desire has been to preserve their own religion while continuing to be Hungarians, and only Hungarians? As witnesses on our behalf we call the battlefields of the War for Independence, the swamps of Volhynia and the rocks of Carso. In the trenches no one ever asked us about our religion. We cannot be separated from Hungary, whose language is our language, whose history is our life. Just like our co-religionists, who still after centuries of exile, have held on to their Spanish language, culture, and love for their old homeland, we will remain vigilant in pursuit of our legitimation and the resurrection of Hungary.

The Parliamentary debate was punctuated by two highly charged emotional episodes for the citizens of Budapest. One day in January, the gallery reserved for the public filled up with Jewish officers from the army reserve. There were several hundred of them, all dressed in uniform, complete with their medals and decorations, and a black mourning patch. They remained standing during the entire day's debate, in solemn and silent protest against the new laws.

A few days later, on February 3, 1939, a group of militants from the pro-Nazi Arrow Cross Party unleashed an armed attack on the faithful who were leaving the Dohány Street Temple after the Saturday prayer service. They threw grenades into the crowd. There were several deaths and many wounded, the large majority of whom were old people.

The laws passed, again over the opposition of the churches that were able to obtain numerous amendments in favor of converted Jews.

But in the meantime Europe had changed. After the annexation of Austria, Hitler was on the Hungarian border, and now he was also allied with Stalin. The Hungarian pro-Nazis, who in recent years had formed three political parties and were winning a growing consensus, organized street demonstrations to applaud the pact. They marched through the streets of Budapest behind giant portraits, side by side, of Hitler and Stalin. They applauded the German-Soviet Pact, symbol of the "common front of proletarian States against the plutocracies." They applauded the USSR, certain that – now that it had been liberated from the Jewish influence of Trotskyism – it would undertake an anti-Semitic policy even more efficient than that introduced by Germany.

That is what was happening in the streets. For the government's part, the new German-Soviet friendship was translated into various official acts: Moscow's restitution of the flags that had been sequestered in 1848 during battles with Kossuth's revolutionary army; several commercial and trade agreements; and a symbolic ceremony at Lvov, where the tracks of the Magyar and Soviet railroads were united – tracks which would be used, two years later, to carry convoys bound for the extermination camps at Auschwitz and which, already in 1941, were being used to deport unknown Jews from the eastern provinces of Hungary.

In the summer of 1941, as Hitler began the invasion of the Soviet Union, the Hungarian Parliament approved the third anti-Semitic law prohibiting marriages between Jews and Christians and providing for sanctions in cases of sexual relations between Jews and Christians outside the bonds of matrimony.

Commonly referred to as the "law for the defense of the race," it treated Judaism like tuberculosis. It was prohibited for couples to marry without showing a medical certificate attesting to the absence of TB, and it was now prohibited for Jews to marry Christians. But while Koch's bacillus could be detected under a microscope, the concept of "Jew" turned out to be not so easy to define. Were the Christian children of the forty thousand mixed marriages celebrated in the past forty years also Jews? Was it just to deprive these two hundred thousand people of the right to marry? What were they supposed to be called: converts? half-bloods? *Halbjuden*? Did race differences survive baptism? Was baptism the cure for the bacillus of Judaism?

The debate went on for months in both houses, and the text of the law was amended many times. The representatives of the National Liberal Party opposed the law for its lack of an "ethical foundation and human justification." The right marshaled its strongest arguments against mixed marriages, which allowed Jews to make their way up the social pyramid, threatening the integrity of "Magyar morality." They cited the pernicious influence of Jewish cinema, theater, music and literature and told of young girls born to illustrious families who felt ashamed if they weren't able to "recite at least two hundred and thirty-five Hebrew aphorisms." Steadfast opposition to the law came from the representatives of the Christian churches in the Chamber of Nobles. According to Cardinal Giustiano Seredi, Prince and Primate of the Hungarian Catholic Church, the state was interfering in areas which should be left up to God, and assimilation was a process that should be encouraged rather than rejected. The Calvinist bishop, László Ravasz, declared sharply that "no biological or chemical formula will ever provide a satisfactory explanation of spiritual or psychological phenomena, such as faith, honesty, justice, the spirit of self-sacrifice, or their opposites," and he reaffirmed that "the Sacred Scriptures teach that the sacrament of baptism brings about spiritual rebirth without regard to sex, age, nationality or physical health." The Bishop of the Lutheran Church, Dr. Béla Kapi, rejected a law that was "in open contrast with the principles of my Church."

In the end, the law passed. For many in Hungary, the law represented the lowering of the threshold of morality, the ethical bankruptcy of the Hungarian people. But those prelates and nobles in the Chamber of Nobles who opposed the law were the only people to do so publicly in the whole of Europe. After passage, perhaps from remorse, perhaps due to the difficulties of implementation, it was agreed that the law that treated the Jews as the equivalent of Koch's bacillus would not go into effect for two years.

Perlasca arrived in Hungary in the middle of that two-year hiatus, a period of uncertainty suspended in a simmering mixture of hatred, embarrassment and unconsciousness, that would boil over the following year. He arrived just as the war was about to end, just at the point when the proponents of Nazism realized that their weeks were numbered. That is when the city of Budapest ceased to be a city, and nobody had the authority any longer to make people listen. Everyone saw what was happening, but nobody intervened. The only ones left to author appeals, take action to avoid mass slaughter or procure food were a dozen or so "strangers," diplomats of nations that had declared their neutrality in the war.

Giorgio Perlasca, who had arrived in Budapest at the end of a long journey away from the war, now found himself at its vortex. He had the opportunity to escape, and he did not. Instead, he became one of those diplomats. One of the most effective.

With just one difference: No one had given him that mandate. He was not an ambassador nor a consul nor a chargé d'affaires. He was simply an employee of the AIB company, a long way from home.

Endnote

1. *New York Times* (July 28, 1979), p. 17.

IV
Before the World's Distracted Eyes

In April 1943, just a few days after he had met with the Romanian leader, Marshal Ion Antonescu, Hitler summoned Admiral Horthy to a meeting at Klessheim castle, near Salzburg. The war on the eastern front was going from bad to worse. The German divisions that had been sent to invade the Soviet Union had been stopped, and then suffered a series of humiliating defeats. Hungary and Romania were no longer considered solid allies of the Axis, and, in Berlin, rumors of their possible defection in the near future were more and more frequent.

In his meeting with Horthy, Hitler, accompanied by Goebbels and von Ribbentrop, was as direct and brutal as ever. He began by accusing the Hungarians of not putting up a real fight on the eastern front. Horthy responded by citing the casualty figures for the Hungarian army: 146,000 killed and 30,000 wounded, plus the loss of 36,000 Jewish workers who had been mobilized and sent into combat against the Bolsheviks. Hitler then moved on to the Jewish question, railing at the admiral for being too soft on the Jews. He accused the Jews of having been the cause of the First World War. He reminded Horthy that it had been the Jews who had tried to bring the Bolshevik revolution to Hungary with the Republic of Béla Kun, and informed him that the Jews in Budapest were providing the Allies with ground information for their bombing missions over the city.

The admiral's rebuttal was no less direct. He reminded Hitler that there were two hundred thousand more Jews in Hungary than there were in Germany when the Nazis took power ten years earlier. He repeated for his ally what he was fond of saying candidly to everyone: "The Hungarians are a noble people, a nation of gentlemen who have thought for over a thousand years that managing money is a dirty activity. It is a job that we have always left up to the Jews, with the result that now, if it weren't for them, the Hungarian economy would collapse. We can try to keep them out of positions of public authority, and we have done that with three successive anti-Semitic laws, but we can't do any more than that."

"What are we supposed to do?" the admiral asked. "Should we liquidate them, kill them all? Apart from any other considerations, it would be an impossible task."

Hitler didn't understand the reasons for the admiral's hesitancy. "It's not necessary to kill them," he explained. "All you have to do is send them to concentration camps or to forced labor in the mines." Horthy didn't agree: "We can't do anything more than we've done already. We've deprived them of their means of support; we certainly can't beat them to death!" Von Ribbentrop entered the discussion to remind Germany's insensitive ally that he had only two possible choices: "either destroy them or send them to concentration camps." Hitler was more specific: "The Jews are parasites. You have to do what they did in Poland. Jews who refuse to work should be shot, while those who are not able to work should be left to die." Then he expounded for Admiral Horthy his well-known theory: "The Jews are like the tuberculosis bacillus; they're contagious. You must not allow yourself to be moved by compassion because, even in nature, innocent creatures, like rabbits and deer, must be decimated if necessary to prevent further destruction. And the Jews are even worse, because they're trying to bring us under Bolshevik domination. Remember that nations that fail to eliminate the Jews are destined to perish."

Admiral Horthy stuck to his guns. At the end of the meeting, Goebbels wrote in his diary, "Horthy is tied to the Jews through his family. . . . He pulled out a lot of humanitarian excuses. The Führer gave it everything he had, but he was able to convince him only in part."

In July of the same year, English and American troops landed on the coast of Sicily, meeting very little resistance as they began their occupation of Italy. On July 25, after the Grand Council of Fascism voted to replace the Duce, King Vittorio Emanuele III dismissed Mussolini and had him arrested. The Fascist Party was dissolved, and Marshal Pietro Badoglio was named as head of the new government. On September 8, 1943, in the midst of the generalized disbandment of the Italian army, Badoglio announced an armistice. In a few days' time, hundreds of thousands of Italian soldiers – on the eastern front, in the Balkans and in Greece – were arrested by their former German allies who began deporting them to Germany.

On the evening of September 8, the Italian businessman, Giorgio Perlasca, was eating dinner in a lovely restaurant on Margarita Island in Budapest when a waiter gave him the news: "You Italians are lucky. For you the war is over." Perlasca phoned the Italian ambassador, Filippo Anfuso. His orders from Rome, very vague, were to "defend the interests of the realm." During the night, Perlasca managed to stop twelve freight cars of livestock before they got to the German border, and in the morning he went to the bank to stop payment on the purchase.

For the 2,500 Italians then in Hungary, the next few days were a time for decisions. The majority were soldiers, divided between those sent to dig trenches at Fort Györ and those who accepted hospitality from some Hungarian family while they waited to see what would happen. Among the civilians, the majority sided with the king and Badoglio. But not Ambassador

Filippo Anfuso. Once he received the news of Mussolini's liberation from prison at Gran Sasso, Anfuso closed the embassy to "traitors" and placed it under the surveillance of the SS. Officials at the Italian Cultural Institute, on the other hand, announced their opposition to Mussolini's new Republic of Salò, and the Hungarian police defended the Institute from an attack by Italian fascists. Thus, for a period of several weeks, there were two rival Italian legations, and the Hungarian government did not know which to treat as legitimate. Anfuso soon left for Berlin to work directly for the Nazis, and, in December, the Republic of Salò sent its own ambassador to Budapest, Raffaele Casertano. For Giorgio Perlasca, and for other people like him, life was becoming complicated, torn between the ever-increasing danger of being deported and the hope, that almost never came true, of obtaining a visa for entry into allied-occupied southern Italy.

At the beginning of 1944, Hungary found itself in the middle of the war. The Red Army continued to advance and was now nearing Galicia, while by now, after Italy's decision to abandon the war, it seemed certain that Budapest was planning a similar move. In diplomatic circles and military command centers in both Budapest and Berlin, it was no secret that the Hungarian Prime Minister, Count Kalláy, was meeting more and more frequently with the British and the Americans to try and negotiate a separate peace.

On March 18, Hitler again summoned Horthy to Klessheim castle and ordered him to name a government loyal to Germany and to strip Count Kalláy of his powers. Horthy was forced to accept. On the same day, eight German divisions crossed the border into Hungary, on a mission of "fraternal aid." With the support of the Hungarian army and police, the German soldiers began arresting opposition leaders of all colors and stripes, from conservative aristocrats to social democrat parliamentarians, and, of course, Jews. Former Prime Minister Kalláy took refuge in the diplomatic headquarters of Turkey. Along with the German troops crossing over into Hungary were members of the

Sondereinsatzkommando (Special Operations Group) led by
Lieutenant Colonel Adolf Eichmann, who had been charged
three years earlier with responsibility for the operational aspects
of the "final solution to the Jewish question." They entered Budapest in a column over a mile long and established their headquarters at the Hotel Hungary.

Of the millions of Jews who had been living in Europe just
four years earlier, the only ones left, by spring 1944, were the
seven hundred thousand who were residents of Hungary. The
others had already been exterminated, beginning with those in
Greater Germany and moving on to those in Serbia, Croatia, Poland, France and Holland. After September 1943, Jews from
northern and central Italy were also included. The significance
of the German occupation of Hungary with the ostentatious
presence of Eichmann could not have been more clear: It was
now time for the Hungarians to take their place on the calendar
for the extermination of the European Jews. And the operation
would have to be taken care of rapidly because, with each passing week, the outcome of the war looked more and more certain
to be a victory for the Allies.

Everything the world needed to know about the Nazis' plans
for the Jews was already known. Two years before, the Apostolic Nuncio in Bratislava, Monsignor Giuseppe Burzio, had
provided the Vatican with accounts reporting that Jews deported
toward the East were being "gassed." For at least two years, the
use of Zyklon B gas was a known fact, as were a lot of details
about the construction of the concentration camps and the ovens
used for cremating the bodies. First-hand news – eyewitness testimony about the daily atrocities carried out in the Warsaw
Ghetto and on the trains that left daily for the extermination
camps – had arrived in London as early as 1942. In April 1943,
news arrived of the armed insurrection of the Jews in the Warsaw Ghetto, which was followed, after several days of fighting,
by the total destruction of the Ghetto at the hands of SS General
Stroop. In July 1943, from his post as Apostolic Delegate in Is-

tanbul, Monsignor Angelo Roncalli (later Pope John XXIII) sent the Vatican a note affirming that "millions of Jews had been sent to Poland and annihilated there," a fact which he also denounced in no uncertain terms to the German ambassador, Franz von Papen. Around this same time, he used his offices to obtain permission for a ship full of Jewish children to cross the Dardanelles Strait and dock in a neutral haven. Well aware of what was happening, he kept in close contact with Zionist organizations, and as early as the beginning of 1944 he was working on behalf of the Jews in Hungary.

In early 1944, representatives of the Polish resistance supplied the Allies with maps of the concentration camps and indications of the rail lines used to transport people to Birkenau. They begged the Allied air forces to bring a halt to the deportations by bombarding rail stations and tracks. They asked that Allied airplanes drop millions of leaflets over Germany informing the German people about what was happening and threatening reprisals. Nothing, absolutely nothing, of what was proposed was carried out or even attempted. There was no military or strategic plan which took into account the "variable" of the extermination then in progress; the programmed deadlines of a war that was proceeding with success were not modified. To the Nazis, those millions of Jews were living people to be killed; to the Allies, they were already dead.

On the morning of March 14, Giorgio Perlasca was awakened in his room at the Blue Danube rooming house by his friend, Professor D'Alessandro. "The Germans are in town. You'd better get out of here, because they want to arrest you."

Perlasca made the rounds of Budapest, sleeping in a different place each night. The city had changed; German soldiers had taken possession of the streets. In the center of town, he saw a boy about ten years old as he ran and then fell down, hit by a rifle shot. He went over near the boy's body, together with some other people, and asked what had happened. A man answered succinctly, "He was a Jew."

On April 5, the newspapers and the radio carried the news that Jews were now required to wear a clearly visible yellow star on their clothes. He saw men and women walking down the streets being insulted and manhandled. He didn't know where to go, and he knew they were looking for him.

"The rumors going around were really ugly," recalls Perlasca, "nobody knew just what to do. I remember one guy I knew, his name was Turolla, who was the representative of Stock brandy of Trieste. At first he slept in different places around town and then after a few days, he went back to his house, thinking he was safe. But instead, they arrested him. I saw him again after the war. They had taken him off to Mauthausen, and the man I had known was nothing but skin and bones."

But Perlasca had a document with him that turned out to be useful: a certificate that he had been given in Barcelona before he went back home after the Spanish Civil War. The paper said, "Dear Brother-in-Arms, no matter where you are in the world, you can turn to Spain." So Perlasca called at the Spanish embassy, directed by first secretary Angel Sanz Briz. They put him up in a villa with extra-territorial status. There were a number of other refugees there including the Countess Dessewffy, whose husband, a member of Parliament, had headed for the hills. They were the owners of "Kis Ujsag," one of Budapest's most important dailies. Angel Sanz Briz was very kind to him. Perlasca stayed at the villa for ten days, during which time he looked into the possibility of obtaining a pass that would allow him to get to southern Italy. But that wasn't possible, so he decided to turn himself in to be sent into internment like the other Italians, diplomats and government officials, who had been working there in Hungary.

That's how he got to the internment camp in Kékes and, when he thinks about it, Perlasca cannot help but smile. "It was a wonderful place. They fed us well, gave us cigarettes to smoke. The people treated us really well." And his wife, as she listens to him tell about it, adds, "Yeah, and they even sang my husband a little song: *'Perlasca, Perlasca, ogni donna ci ricasca.'"* (Perlasca, Perlasca, the women are yours for the askin'.)

Budapest had become unrecognizable. The new government had finally begun to take effective action to "resolve" – in line with the Germans' wishes – "the Jewish question in Hungary." Amid a generalized silence, daily convoys, organized by Eichmann, left the eastern provinces for the extermination camps in Poland. The Jews from the villages who managed to escape sought refuge in the capital which was thought to be the last safe port. They came to the city by any means of transportation they could find, still dressed in their country outfits and, frightened and disoriented, often fell prey immediately to the Nyilas bands. They spoke in strict dialect, and they had no idea where to hide.

Every day from the Hotel Hungary, Eichmann dictated his conditions to the Jewish Council: Money to be delivered within hours, buildings to be evacuated, lists of able-bodied men and women to be sent to Germany to contribute to the war effort. The Council collaborated. Throughout the city you could see columns of men leaving on foot, bound for Vienna or for the mines of Croatia. At the beginning of the summer, it was decided that the Jews of Budapest were to move, within forty-eight hours, into selected buildings with a big yellow star painted on the front door. English and Swiss newspapers receiving reports from Budapest saw this follow-up measure to the earlier order requiring stars on clothes as a clear signal that deportation was about to begin.

On June 16, in the presence of numerous German military officers and civilian officials, a bonfire was held in Budapest to burn books written by Jewish authors, Hungarian and foreign. The government had prepared a detailed list, giving book stores, libraries, schools and other institutions fifteen days to deliver the books. The list contained one hundred and twenty Hungarian authors and one hundred and thirty foreigners. Some 444,627 books were collected, enough to fill twenty-two freight cars.

They were unloaded in the middle of the square and burned to the sound of applause; Hungary was finally freeing itself from the malevolent influence of Judaism. The ceremony was filmed. The fire burned on for hours: books of literature and medicine, politics, the abhorrent theories of psychoanalysis, poetry anthologies. Just a few blocks away from Paul Street, Ferenc Molnár's *Paul Street Boys* also burned. Among books by Italian authors, they burned the works of Guido da Verona, who was extremely popular in Budapest.

During the summer, the worst rumors began to spread. Escapees from the eastern provinces told about the deportations and the mass killings, but their listeners were city people who weren't prepared to believe their stories, or who said that whatever had happened in the countryside, couldn't happen in the capital, an open city, full of foreigners, of officials from the Red Cross and the diplomatic legations of the neutral countries. The city was bombed several times by Allied planes, and the Nyilas and the German command spread the word that the pilots had been given information about the targets by the city's Jews. The Soviet Army was advancing across the plains, accompanied by stories of pillage and rape. But, in any case, the end of the war depended on them, since there was no hope of the Americans getting that far from the western front. Budapest was living on the edge of the abyss, but it was still pretending that it wasn't. On Sundays, the season's soccer matches continued to be played according to schedule, and the famous nightclubs and cafés along the Danube were jam-packed. At the Arizona, night after night, the dancing girls wrapped themselves around the chandeliers and swung down through the tables.

For their part, the wealthy Jews of Budapest did little or nothing to warn the rest of the community of the coming danger, even though the members of the Jewish Council appointed by Eichmann were well-informed about what was happening. Samuel Stern, the head of the Council, had heard personally the tale told by two prisoners who had escaped from Auschwitz. In May,

Rudolph Kasztner, one of the leaders of the Zionist organization, was informed directly by Dieter Wisliceny, Eichmann's vice-commander, of the decision to carry out the "total deportation" of the Hungarian Jews. Other leading members of the community had known for a long time about the fate of the Jews in Slovakia and in Poland.

And yet the Jewish Council collaborated, in the illusion that "Budapest was different." And then, between May and June, between official meetings at the Hotel Hungary and semi-clandestine encounters at the Arizona club, Eichmann's SS and various members of the Jewish community conducted a series of obscure, improvised negotiations involving the wealthiest part of the Jewish population – money in exchange for lives. A list was drawn up of 1,700 wealthy Jews from Budapest who Eichmann was willing to allow to leave for Switzerland upon payment of $1,000 each. There was another plan to ransom Jews from Budapest in exchange for trucks for the German army. Money was paid in exchange for favored treatment in the concentration camps.

The most sensational episode, which came out only after the war, involved a group of the capital's most important families: the Chorin and Mauthner families, and the Barons Kornfeld and Weiss, the owners of the big "Manfred Weiss" steel mill on the island of Cspel, as well as other important steel mills, some bauxite mines, and an airplane factory. Just after their arrival in Budapest, Eichmann's men kidnapped several women members of these families and took them to Vienna. Then they announced that they were ready to deal. Within six weeks, lawyers for the four families on one side, and for Eichmann and Himmler on the other, came to the following agreement: ownership of the entire industrial complex, which employed some forty thousand people, passed under the control of the SS, represented by Colonel Kurt Becher, Himmler's financial agent. In exchange, the SS authorized the departure of forty-six members of the four families (thirty-eight Jews and eight Christians) for Switzerland and Portugal.

It was decided that the exiles would receive compensation in the amount of $600,000 and DM 250,000, with a 5 percent commission for Kurt Becher. The agreement, overseen personally by Hitler in Berlin, was signed on May 17, 1944, when the deportation of the Jews from the eastern provinces was in full swing. That same morning, wearing disguises and carrying false documents, the forty-six family members left by train for Vienna. There, nine of them were held hostage to ensure that the agreement would not be revealed. On June 25, on board two special Lufthansa flights, the group was flown to Lisbon, where the only public news of the whole affair came out; a news dispatch from Reuters announced the arrival in Lisbon of a "group of Hungarian millionaires." Of the $600,000 promised as compensation, the SS deducted two-thirds for "unforseen expenses."

By this time what was happening in Hungary could not be hidden any longer. President Franklin Roosevelt, Pope Pius XII, John Cardinal Spellman of New York, and the King of Sweden sent explicit messages to Horthy, publicly putting him on notice to stop the persecution of the Jews. On July 7, when some 440,000 Jews from the provinces had already been deported, Horthy ordered that the deportations be stopped. On July 18, the regent proposed an emigration plan providing for 13,000 Jews to go to Switzerland, 10,000 children to Sweden, 5,000 Jews to the United States, and for the issuance of transit permits allowing the emigrants to reach Palestine by way of the Balkans with the permission of the Romanian, Bulgarian, and Turkish governments. Both the United States and Britain reacted feebly, the latter visibly preoccupied by the prospect of further emigration to Palestine which might upset the equilibrium of its protectorate. This despite the almost daily news reports, from BBC broadcasts and United Press dispatches to articles in the *New York Times* that described the extermination of the Hungarian Jews as "imminent" or "already in progress." On July 24, the Red Army liberated the concentration camp at Majdánka, on the outskirts of Lublin, and found there what the Nazis had not had time to destroy: some barracks, a cremation oven, and a gas chamber, completely intact. For the first time the world had concrete proof of the real meaning of "the voyage of the Jews."

On August 1, the *New York Times* carried an article published without any particular fanfare on page 17 :

> Declaring its fear that by the time the war has been won the largest part of the Jewish population of Europe will have been extinguished, a mass meeting of 40,000 American Jews gathered in Madison Square Park yesterday afternoon adopted a resolution embodying a program for saving as many Jews in the Nazi-occupied territories as possible.
>
> The huge crowd, standing closely packed for more than two hours despite the oppressive heat, heard messages from President Roosevelt and Governor Dewey expressing their abhorrence at the atrocities against the Jews in Europe. . . . The mass meeting . . . attracted a throng that filled Madison Avenue solidly from Twenty-third to Twenty-fifth Streets; extended down the side streets and packed the walks of Madison Square Park . . .

The purpose of the demonstration, organized by the American Jewish Conference, was to put pressure on the president to accept Horthy's plan and, above all, not to be stingy about granting visas to Jews wishing to enter the United States, and to set up "free ports" (camps to welcome and sort out refugees) in Turkey to allow Jews from the Balkan peninsula to reach Palestine. But President Roosevelt hesitated to take even these obvious measures, for reasons which were not very noble. He feared, in fact, that a policy openly favorable to European Jews could harm his chances for re-election in November. He was afraid of opposition to a policy in favor of immigration, and of stirring up an already existent anti-Semitism that was not all that latent. Among the many who protested against and emphasized the gravity of such an attitude was the writer I. F. Stone, who described the situation in an article for *The Nation*:

> There are people here who say the President can't risk a move of this kind before election. I believe that an insult to the American people. I don't believe any but a few unworthy bigots would object to giving a few thousand refugees a temporary breathing spell in their flight from oppression. It is a question of Mr. Roosevelt's courage and good faith. All he is called upon to do, after all, is what Franco did months ago, yes, *Franco*. Franco established "free ports", internment camps, for refugees who fled across his border, refugees, let us remember, from his own ally and patron, Hitler. Knowing the Führer's maniacal hatred for Jews, that kindness on Franco's part took considerably more courage than Mr. Roosevelt needs to face a few sneering editorials, perhaps, from the "Chicago Tribune." I say "perhaps", because I do not know that even Colonel McCormick would in fact be hostile.[1]

The Allies' failure to do much for the Hungarian Jews was an invitation to the Red Cross and the diplomatic representatives of the neutral powers in Budapest to strengthen their efforts and to become more active. The only result worthy of note, however, was an initiative of the King of Sweden. On July 9, 1944, an unusual young man named Raoul Wallenberg, a member of one of Sweden's wealthiest families, arrived in Hungary. With no prior diplomatic experience, he had accepted with enthusiasm an assignment that was as dramatic as it was vague: Do whatever it takes – pay, promise, bribe – to save the greatest possible number of Hungarian Jews. The money came from Jewish organizations and American labor unions.

The population of Budapest knew next to nothing about all these negotiations, much less Perlasca, still isolated in the "little oasis" of the internment camp at Kékes. In the fall, however, rumors of war started to arrive there as well. The group of Italians was divided in two, and Perlasca was transferred to Cakanydorozlo together with some others, under the supervision of an officer of the military police. They were still well-treated, but they were more worried than ever about the future. Many of them figured that the advance of the Soviet troops would end up with the Italian internees being dragged off to Germany, just like the Italian soldiers who had been deported after the September 8 armistice was announced. The Germans considered them traitors and accused them openly of having too many privileges.

So on October 13, Perlasca and three other friends decided to try to escape to Budapest on the evening train. But that proved not to be necessary. Perlasca managed to make his way out of the internment camp aboard one of the cars of the Swedish diplomatic delegation; a telegram from the Ministry of Internal Affairs had arrived, granting Signor Giorgio Perlasca permission for a fifteen-day stay in Budapest for some clinical examinations. After a five-hour ride, they arrived in the capital at night and, passing in front of the castle, they noticed something strange: The soldiers guarding Admiral Horthy's residence were carrying machine guns.

"That means Horthy has signed the armistice with the Allies," they commented. An armistice, with the German army occupying the city.

One month earlier, on September 15, a distinguished civil engineer had paid a visit to the Castle. Dr. Ottó Komoly was the President of the Hungarian Zionist Association, President of the Red Cross's International Committee on Jewish Affairs, and a member of the Jewish Council. He was one of the few Jews who could still move about fairly freely. Perfectly up to date about what was happening, he had been negotiating for months with anyone he thought might be useful, trying desperately to find some way to save the Hungarian Jews. That day he had succeeded in getting an appointment with Miklós Horthy, Jr., the

Admiral's son, whose anti-Nazi sentiments were well-known. The proposal that Komoly wished to present was a realistic one: the appointment, without a lot of publicity, of a government commissioner charged with carrying out the progressive elimination of the excesses introduced by the anti-Semitic laws, so as to gradually recreate the conditions for co-existence between Jews and other Hungarians. Miklós Horthy said the proposal was interesting and asked Komoly to prepare a written text. Then he asked if he could speak to him in confidence. The ensuing dialogue between the Zionist leader and the Hungarian nobleman was later transcribed by Komoly into his diary.

Horthy began by saying, "I am anti-Semitic by birth and education. I couldn't be otherwise, given the way we talked about the Jews in our house. It's inconceivable, for example, that I could marry a Jewish woman or that my children could have Jewish blood. But you see, as I grew older, I became involved in the economic life of the country. I owned a firm, for example, that was unable to obtain an export license from the ministry. And then along comes one of the many Groszs or Kohns and they get the license right away. So why didn't they give us a license? It's simple. Because the official at the ministry who earns 600 pengö a month probably said, 'for what they pay me, I don't want any headaches. So what if they get a license? There's nothing in it for me.' And then the Jew comes along and hands him a little bit of money so he can go out and have a night on the town, and before you know it, he's got a license. You see, our civil servants aren't the least bit concerned about the country's economic interests. If it were up to them, the country would go bankrupt. That's why we need the Jews. And the Jews, by looking out for their own interests, have also advanced the country's interests. . . . And look at the mess we're in now. We've made a lot of mistakes, including mistakes on the Jewish question. We should never have allowed things to get to this point."

Komoly admitted that the Jews had also made some mistakes of their own but that they had to be understood in the context of two thousand years of oppression. At which point, young Horthy started up again: "Sure, sure. Everybody hated the Jews, but at the same time everybody had a Jew in the house, and he was the one who knew how to make things work."

He began to act out a scene, changing his voice as he changed roles. "'At your service, Signor Count, what can I do for you?' 'Ah, you're back again, you stinking Jew. Take care of this for me, and take care of that!' And so the Jew took care of everything, and the Count went on living the good life without having to worry about anything at all. Sure, sure, not all nobles are like that. Some of them are very good people. . . . But then the situation changed. The Jew became rich, and the Count was in trouble. He could no longer afford to change his shirt collar every day, while in the meantime the Jew had bought himself a beautiful house. Now it was the Count who went to the Jew's house when the Jew decided to give a party. It's only natural that hatred for the Jews spread throughout the country."

Then Komoly told Horthy, Jr., about the fundamentals of Zionism and the ideal of a homeland in Palestine and sounded him out about the possibility of favoring Jewish emigration to Palestine. Horthy interrupted him: "We need the Jews. I'm an athlete, and I know that new records are set only when there's competition. The Hungarian needs the stimulus provided by the Jew, and emigration will have to be regulated according to the needs of the nation. If we do things right, it will take us one or two generations to teach the Hungarians how to manage the economy, just like the English aristocracy learned how to do it."

Horthy then politely said good-bye and assured him that he would read the proposal very carefully. But then he added, "By now it's too late. I don't think we'll be able to do anything to save the situation."

Three days later, on Hitler's personal instructions, Major Otto Skorzeny, the same man who had freed Mussolini from Gran

Sasso the year before, was given orders to eliminate Miklós Horthy, Jr. – thought to be an important leader in the anti-Nazi resistance, in contact with Jewish leaders and emissaries from Yugoslavia's Marshal Josip Tito – and to prepare the way for the men of the Arrow Cross to take power.

In the early morning hours of October 15, the day chosen by Admiral Horthy to announce the armistice with the Soviets, a squad of men under Skorzeny's command broke into the royal palace and captured Miklós Horthy, Jr. After some violent exchanges around the palace grounds, Horthy, Jr., was taken away – some say he was rolled up inside a carpet. Despite the kidnapping of his son, old Admiral Horthy kept his promise and broadcast a brief message on the radio announcing that the Axis had lost the war and that the Hungarians would no longer join in combat against the Red Army.

Endnote

1. *The Nation* (June 10, 1944), pp. 670–71.

V

The Bogus Spanish Consul

The announcement of the armistice was broadcast on the radio by Admiral Miklós Horthy at one o'clock. Ten minutes later, the news that the war was over began to spread throughout the city. At the soccer stadium, in the Ferencvaros district, thousands of people were on hand for the soccer match against Ujpest. When the announcement of the regent's message came over the public address system, the players gathered in the center of the field and the spectators rose to their feet. The game was suspended, and the celebration had already begun as the crowd made its way out of the stadium. But more than any place else, it was in the "houses with the yellow star" that an uncontrollable sense of euphoria began to spread. Front yards filled to overflowing as people danced for joy and ripped the yellow stars off their clothes.

Five hours later, the euphoria gave way to panic. SS units took control of the city's nerve centers, and the armed bands of the Arrow Cross Party began to advance on their objectives. Major László Ferenczy occupied the radio station and broadcast over and over the following appeal: "In the face of the eternal Russian threat and for the preservation of Christianity and Western civilization, Hungary shall carry on its struggle side by side with our German comrades in arms." That evening the announcement was made that Major Ferenc Szálasi, leader of the Arrow Cross Party, had proclaimed himself regent for the purpose of continuing the war, and that he would soon be forming a new government. This was followed by a series of further announcements. Another statement from Horthy, obviously extracted under pressure, gave his approval of the formation of the new government under Szálasi and announced his own departure from Hungary. Another message declared the constitution of a "Tribunal for the Rendering of Accounts," which would provide for the execution of "traitors" and "subversives"; still another message directed the immediate assignment of fifty thousand men to the German army for the construction of fortifications around Vienna. Finally it was announced that the defense of the capital against the combined Soviet-Romanian advance would continue under the command of the German army.

Horthy's surrender symbolized the end of the old Hungary. The aging admiral, who had signed the declaration of the armistice despite his son's kidnapping, put on his dress uniform and pinned all of his medals in place. Then, surrounded by his court, he sat down on his throne and awaited the arrival of the SS. The royal guards responded to the attack with armed resistance and were massacred.

That evening, at the royal palace in Buda, Major Ferenc Szálasi was installed as the new Head of State. He ordered that he be addressed as "Brother Leader" or "Guide of the Race." Formerly an army officer relegated to service in a garrison on the outskirts of the city, he had become the leader of the Arrow Cross Party, named after the symbol of the crown of St. Stephen, which was shot through with arrows, and very similar to the Hitlerian swastika. He chose a green shirt as the party uniform, and he showed the admiration for Hitler that was due to the "designated leader of the newly born European community." The first point of the party platform was: "to combat on the east against the Marxist dictatorship led by the Jews, and to combat on the west the dictatorship of the plutocracy, also led by the Jews"; it then went on to speak of the corporatization of society, expropriation of the National Bank, agrarian reform, the "magyarization" of social and cultural life, and "creation of the Great Danubian Carpathian Fatherland."

Following the thread of Szálasi's reasoning was often difficult for his own supporters. "Brother Leader" was often possessed by mystic crises and sprinkled his speeches with religious invocations and requests for benediction for his crusade against the Jews and the Bolsheviks. But, in the last five years, this mixture of visible insanity and grim proposals had brought about a steady increase in the popularity of the Arrow Cross. The Hungarian Nazi Party had been gaining support not only among low-ranking army officers but also among the factory workers, miners, and farmers who, only ten years earlier, had been the heart of the electorate of the Social Democratic Party. Even many of the steelworkers who had organized a series of ever-more-successful strikes at the Csepel plant had joined the "Nyilas," as had many of the soldiers who had come back from service on the Russian front, low-level bureaucrats in the offices of the capital, and unemployed university graduates. Giorgio Perlasca, like everybody else in the capital, followed the developments of the military takeover on the radio. He had taken refuge in the house of a Hungarian friend who had fled the capital. On the morning of the 16th, a young girl came to the house to do the cleaning. She told Perlasca how enthusiastic she was about the Nazis and the Nyilas, and that she was ready to do anything to give them a hand. Perlasca realized that his friend's house was no longer safe for him. He went outside and saw the dead bodies lying in the street. In Király street, one of the neighborhoods where the "houses with the yellow star" had been attacked by the Nyilas, a group of Jews had barricaded themselves in a house and returned the enemy fire. But the battle ended quickly, and the Jews lost.

Perlasca did not know where to go, and he was not feeling very steady on his legs. He was able to get himself to the house of his friend D'Alessandro, who had also reached the capital. He had a high fever and was taken to the Pajor clinic where he was treated for a serious intestinal infection. But the clinic was not safe either. Police came into the wards every day looking for dissidents and checking documents. Somebody got into his locker and stole his bag where he had hidden some money. At that point, he decided to leave the clinic and convinced the doorman of the Blue Danube rooming house to give him a room. The next day he got a room at the Hotel Hungary. It was full of German soldiers.

"It was dangerous," he says. "But at least there was a restaurant and a café. I was able to get some rest, and it was there that I got the idea to go back to Sanz Briz and ask for help." He went over to the Spanish embassy and asked to be given a set of Spanish documents. Sanz Briz hesitated. He claimed that he could not issue the documents without first getting approval from the government in Madrid.

> That's when I started yelling at him. 'Can't you see what's happening in this city?' I said. 'Can't you see that they're murdering women and children, that they're torturing people and putting innocent people in jail?' Sanz Briz, as a good Latin, understood. Fifteen minutes later I had a regular Spanish passport and a letter, addressed to the Hungarian Ministry of Internal Affairs, where it was written that on October 13, 1944, the Spanish Head of State had granted my request for Spanish citizenship, which I had made some two years earlier. My baptismal name was now Jorge.
>
> Sanz Briz then asked me to stay on at the embassy office and help out with the effort to protect the Jews. I was happy about it. I was glad to be able to do something useful. I had them fill out a certificate identifying me as a member of the embassy staff. And that's how I started my work.

In October 1944, Budapest was destined to be the next city engulfed by the Holocaust. The only thing that could keep it from happening was the rapid arrival of the Soviet army and the consequent Nazi retreat. In the meantime, help could come only from a small group of people made up of the staff of the International Red Cross and the diplomats representing neutral countries: Franco's Spain, represented by Angel Sanz Briz and consul general Charles Lutz; Sweden, represented by Minister Carl Ivan Daniellson, who had recently been joined by the special envoy of King Gustav, Raoul Wallenberg; Portugal, represented by honorary consul Count Pongrácz; and the Vatican, represented by the Apostolic Nuncio, Monsignor Angelo Rotta. The International Red Cross was headed by Friederich Born, with the help of a number of prominent families from the Hungarian aristocracy. Between official representatives and staff there were no more than two hundred people.

During the Horthy regime, the diplomats and the Red Cross had had some chance at least to intervene in "hardship cases," with the possibility of putting several thousand Jews under their protection. Now, with the new Szálasi government, everything was becoming more complicated, and much riskier. The day-to-day situation was much harder to keep under control because of the activity of the Nyilas armed bands and the schedule of deportations that were once again in full swing. The only really safe places were the houses which each delegation had been able to obtain for itself and which were being crammed tighter and tighter with Jewish protectees. It was called the "international ghetto," an area near the banks of the Danube, around St. Stephen's Park, where the various delegations rented office space. It was a strange sight: all those doorways, balconies and windows hung with fluttering Swedish, Spanish, Swiss or Portuguese flags, or carrying the Vatican insignia. In front of all the embassies there were endless lines of people who came to request certificates, pieces of paper, anything that might protect them from the will of the armed bands.

The office of the Spanish embassy, in Eötvös street, was under the direction of Madame Tournè, a French woman of Hungarian origin who had been working at the embassy for twenty years. Her staff consisted of her son, Gaston, and ten volunteers, chosen from among the first to apply for Spanish protection. They never left the office. Every application for protection passed through Madame Tournè's hands, while her son kept busy trying to track down and get back Spanish protectees who had been arrested. Sanz Briz examined each application, with advice and counsel from a Hungarian attorney, Zoltán Farkas, legal advisor to the Spanish embassy for the last twenty years, who also functioned as interpreter.

Perlasca started into his new job by visiting the houses in the "international ghetto." At the time, there were no more than three hundred Spanish protectees, but the number was changing daily. After a few days of observation, he started taking some personal initiatives. He went down to police headquarters to protest about a Nyilas band that had broken into one of the protected houses. Then he requested an appointment with József Gera, "Brother Leader" and member of the Szálasi government. That first encounter with Gera turned out to be rather tumultuous. Perlasca started off protesting vigorously that the Nyilas had entered one of the "Spanish houses," thrown an old man out of a fifth floor window, raped a woman and forcefully carried two men away against their will.

"Gera," Perlasca recalls, "went into a real hysterical fit. He started running back and forth across the room, yelling that the Jews were all the same, that they had thrown a bomb into the theater where he was giving a speech, that it was time they should all be exterminated."

Perlasca waited for him to calm down and then illustrated the position of the Spanish government. He explained that the people in the houses were under the protection of a neutral country which maintained friendly relations with Hungary, and that their protection thus had to be guaranteed at all times. Gera sat there listening to him, amazed. Then he asked him, "But why isn't Franco fighting against the Jews?"

Perlasca explained that in Spain there was a hundred-year-old statute that prohibited the recording of a Spanish citizen's religious affiliation on personal documents. Perlasca could see that Gera was even more amazed by this, and he realized that he could go on. He told Gera that before God and nature all beings are equal, and that it was terribly wrong that political hatred was now being exacerbated by racism. Gera didn't interrupt him. Then he commented, "Maybe you're right. Maybe Hitler made a mistake by declaring war against the Jews because, by doing that, he has spread our forces too thin. . . . But by now it is too late, the choice has been made and we have to see it through to the end."

So, it seemed that "Brother Leader" wasn't so sure after all. Perlasca thought he might still have some room to maneuver. Adopting a confidential tone, he explained to Gera that Spain was also protecting the Jews because of the necessity of maintaining a balanced foreign policy. That, in any case, the war would be over soon, and it would again be time for making agreements and showing appreciation. This last word – "appreciation" – Perlasca pronounced very carefully, knowing that he would be striking a sensitive chord.

"And, in fact," Perlasca recalls, "Gera changed his attitude. He let me know how fond he was of Spain and assured me that our protectees would be treated with all due respect. In the end, he shook my hand. I remember how uncomfortable I felt during that handshake. I was shaking hands with a person who could sign a death sentence as easily as he would a greeting card."

The next day, for the first time, he went down to the freight station where the Hungarian military police and the SS were carrying out the deportations. Perlasca was one of those people who have a professional interest in train stations and railroad cars. And those cars were the same as the cars his company used to transport livestock. "Only, we treated the livestock better." The Jews being deported were pushed and shoved up onto the loading docks. Perlasca noticed one old man who had pinned on his chest, next to the yellow star, the medals of honor he had been awarded for service in the First World War. Without thinking about it, he stepped forward, took the man under his arm, and helped him into his car. A German officer signaled one of the Hungarian police to check the papers of that person who was interfering. Perlasca showed him his passport and the letter certifying that he was on the staff of the Spanish embassy. He was allowed to take the man away.

In the middle of November, Sanz Briz, Perlasca, Attorney Farkas and Madame Tournè held a meeting to decide on a line of conduct. The situation in Budapest had reached tragic proportions, and the German surrender was no longer a question of days but of weeks or months. True, the Russians were advancing, but less rapidly than had been expected, and it was impossible to stop the deportations. Day after day, the Jews being "lent" to Germany continued to leave in conditions that everybody was able to observe, on their way to a certain death.

"But there were other things happening too, that were truly scandalous," Perlasca recounts. "Switzerland and Sweden had set up committees at their embassies, in charge of issuing letters of protection, and a horrible commerce had begun. Counterfeit letters were put into circulation and sold at incredibly high prices. I collected the testimony of a number of people who had paid for documents that were completely worthless, and I also had the names of the corrupt embassy officials, and how much they were asking. Everybody knew about it, and so when the Nyilas brutalized Jews who were protected by these false documents, the Swiss and Swedish officials didn't have any moral standing to protest. There was a black market in food as well. On several occasions I myself discovered that food I had bought on the black market actually came from the Red Cross." Conditions in the safe houses themselves were desperately chaotic and disorganized, and the legitimate authorities in the embassies had issued no guidelines or indications of how they should be managed.

Holed up in a room in the Spanish embassy, the little group of people decided to organize themselves. In the first place, they established that letters of protection were to be issued to all persons requesting them, without regard to social status, connections or friendships, and without asking for anything in exchange. To be protected it was sufficient to claim "Sephardic origin" or any degree of family relationship or commercial interests in Spain and, where necessary, the Spanish legation would apply the following principle of law: Given that the Hungarian racial laws denied Jews their legal rights as citizens, the Spanish government assumed the right to grant Jews Spanish citizenship, in unlimited numbers. The letters were all to be backdated to the day before the Szálasi government took power, and were all to follow the same formula: "the X family has requested permission to move to Spain. . . . While awaiting departure, the family shall be under the protection of the Spanish government."

Perlasca proposed that the safe houses – there were eight in all – should be organized as far as possible along military lines. Of those he had visited, one in particular, in Pannonia Street, seemed to him to be a model to follow. It was under the leadership of a retired colonel, a Christian, who could move about freely and warn everyone in case of attack. Inside the house, the colonel had organized everything according to military rules: an early wake-up call, common meals, no arguing about the assignment of physical space to be occupied, a prohibition on leaving the building, even if the official decrees allowed for an hour of leave per day, and a single collection of money to be used for supplies and provisions.

It was also clear, however, that the protection guaranteed by Spain had to go beyond the issuance of the letter. It was essential that the government know that the Spanish were ready to intervene at any time, in response to mistreatment or abuse. The group decided, therefore, to "let themselves be seen" as often as possible, to conduct frequent inspections of the houses and to visit police headquarters and the ministries on a daily basis, leaving something written, something official.

They saved the most delicate question for last. Szálasi and his supporters knew that their days were numbered, and they probably imagined that, in the very likely case of defeat, they would be put on trial. Part of the strategy, then, must be to give them some hope of receiving diplomatic recognition for their government and to let them understand that any humanitarian treatment of the Jews on their part would be taken into account after the war. "They'll ask for official diplomatic recognition from Madrid," Sanz Briz concluded, "and I'm certainly not authorized to grant it. But we've got to handle things in a way that makes them believe it's possible. So we've got to be convincing; talk to them, make promises, but always find some way to delay."

On November 17, Sanz Briz, Farkas and Perlasca attended a meeting of the neutral diplomats. For Perlasca it was a kind of apprenticeship for his diplomatic career. It gave him the opportunity to introduce himself, get to know the people he would be working with and get some understanding of what motivated them and what they were afraid of. The document that came out of that meeting provides a good indication of what the climate was like and what the diplomats thought of their options:

Memorandum

The accredited representatives of the neutral powers in Budapest present, with respect, the following message to the Royal Hungarian Government:

Whereas during the month of August almost half a million Jews were deported from Hungary to foreign countries, and whereas the governments of the neutral countries have reliable information about what such deportation means in real terms, the representatives of the above-mentioned powers adopted, in common agreement, a diplomatic note, addressed to the Royal Hungarian Government, requesting that it prevent the renewal of deportation proceedings.

This diplomatic step, which at the time was favorably received, led to saving the lives of several hundred thousand people.

The day after October 15, the new government, and his Excellency Szálasi in person, issued a declaration according to which there were to be no further deportations, and no extermination of the Jews. Notwithstanding all of this, the representatives of the neutral powers know, from absolutely reliable sources, that it has already been decided to carry out, with rigorous cruelty, the deportation of all the Jews. The entire world is witness to the monstrosity of this operation (small children torn from their mothers, old people and the sick forced to lie on the floor under the practically non-existent roof of a brick factory, men and women left without food for weeks on end, tens of thousands of people crammed into an abandoned brick factory, women raped, others shot on sight for no reason at all, etc.).

Meanwhile, just as it was claimed during the summer, the assertion has now been made again that what we are dealing with are not deportations but transfers due to the necessity of performing work abroad. But the representatives of the neutral powers know full well the horrible reality, for the unfortunate victims, that is hidden behind this justification. The appalling manner with which these transport operations are carried out makes it possible to intuit the tragic end of this exodus.

In the face of these atrocities, the representatives of the neutral powers cannot escape the duty, imposed by humanitarian and Christian sentiments, to express their dismay to the Royal Hungarian Government, and to make the following requests:

1) That the government withdraw the resolution authorizing the deportation of the Jews and suspend the measures enacted so that the poor people who have been removed from their homes can return to their families as soon as possible.

2) That those who, pursuant to the need to perform work abroad, have been forced to live in concentration

camps, be treated humanely (sufficient food and adequate housing, hygiene, religious counseling, respect for life).

3) Total and faithful observance of the measures enacted by the Royal Hungarian Government in favor of the Jews protected by the accredited embassies in Budapest. Instances of non-compliance have been increasing and demonstrate a truly surprising disrespect by subordinate bodies and agencies for the measures handed down by their superior authorities.

The representatives of the neutral powers hope that the Royal Hungarian Government will fully understand the intent of this diplomatic initiative and that, by welcoming it, will return to the full respect and application of the declarations and promises made by his Excellency Szálasi. This initiative was not suggested only by compassion felt for the Jewish victims of persecution, but also by profound respect for Hungary which we should like to see liberated of a stain that could color her glorious history forever. And the government, which is responsible for the well-being of the Hungarian people, will certainly want to protect the nation from the inevitable application of sanctions by the powers at war with Hungary should the deportation and extermination of the Jews be allowed to continue. It should not be forgotten, furthermore, that enemy invaders could resort to the application of the same methods against the Hungarian people.

However this diplomatic step is received by the Hungarian government, the effect of its behavior will inevitably be reflected in no small way in the destiny of its own people. If it should be received favorably, such reception will certainly prove to be useful, above all in the painful eventuality of an enemy invasion, in the service, with increased interest and good will, of the cause of the Hungarian people.

The representatives of the neutral powers are convinced that the noble Hungarian nation, in reference to its own ancient Christian tradition, will want to remain faithful, even in this difficult moment, to the principles and methods that have made Hungary a civilized country, admired throughout the world.

The diplomatic note was signed by Carl Ivan Daniellson of Sweden, Harold Fehler of Switzerland, Monsignor Angelo Rotta, Apostolic Nuncio and Angel Sanz Briz of Spain.

"That document was very important," Perlasca says now. "But I was really puzzled by the way the diplomats worked. It seemed impossible for them to change their habits. It was difficult, for example, to find anyone at work before eleven in the morning. And it was really a struggle to get them to give up the routine of a life consisting of ceremonies, official encounters, salons and receptions. None of them ever visited the houses that had the flag of their country flying over the front door, even though their presence on the scene would have been an enormous help. Only Wallenberg, who was not a diplomat, was able to understand immediately that what counted was not so much the diplomatic notes but activism. The difference between him and the others was, in my view, a certain sense of humanity, a dedication to the honor of his country, which, quite frankly, the others didn't have. He was on a mission. He considered his work a mission. That was the difference."

On November 29, Angel Sanz Briz called Giorgio Perlasca into his office. "Perlasca, I've finished," Sanz Briz told him.

"I'm leaving tomorrow morning. I can't stay in Budapest any longer. The diplomatic recognition game is over. Look here." He showed him a letter from the Hungarian Ministry of Foreign Affairs, calling him to a meeting and enjoining him to move the seat of the diplomatic legation from Budapest to Sopron, near the Austrian border, where part of the Hungarian government had already moved. "If I go to this meeting, they'll ask me if Spain recognizes *de jure* the Szálasi government. And I can't do that. I've been able to keep them hanging for a month and a half, but now the moment of truth has arrived. They won't accept just words anymore, they'll want something in writing, something official. I've got to leave under cover. Because, if I go publicly, then the Szálasi government will consider that diplomatic relations with Spain have been officially interrupted, and they'll close the embassy.

> Listen to me, Perlasca. You have been invaluable, and I appreciate everything you've done. I've been able to get you a German visa. You can leave too. I'm going to Bern, and I can assure you that, from there, I'll make sure you receive a visa that will allow you to cross the border between Germany and Switzerland. Wait here for a few days and then come to Bern. Believe me, unfortunately, there's nothing more we can do here.

Perlasca looked at him, perplexed. "And in the meantime, what am I supposed to do?" he asked.

"Don't do anything special," Sanz Briz advised him. "Wait for the right moment and then come away. Think about it. I'm leaving tomorrow morning."

Perlasca didn't sleep that night. At six in the morning he accompanied Sanz Briz, who was leaving for Switzerland. Then he left the embassy offices and went over to St. Stephen's Park. The police had already started the usual roundup, in a house protected by the Swedish flag. He ran into Major Tarpataky. He was a good person, very humane, who had helped him quite a bit in the past month. He was one of the officers in charge of overseeing the operation of capturing Jews in the park, but if somebody was getting away, he would turn his head, pretending he hadn't seen anything.

"Tarpataky," Perlasca recalls, "was more depressed than usual that day. He told me he was full of anxiety. 'If I don't collaborate with the Nyilas, they'll kill me. If I keep on doing it, as soon as the Russians get here *they'll* kill me, because they'll hold me responsible for all the atrocities. What am I supposed to do?' I tried to console him and assured him that the people would show their appreciation for the way he had behaved. He told me to rest easy; his men would not enter the houses. Then he turned over to me two Jews that his men had captured in the park. 'You take care of them, find a place for them in one of the houses.' "

Perlasca, as he had done every other morning, continued on his rounds of the safe houses. From 35 St. Stephen's Park he went on to 44 and 48 Pannonia Street, then to 5 Phoenix Street. Everything was under control, but the residents already knew that Sanz Briz was gone. They crowded around Perlasca, and they made him swear that he wouldn't leave. "I was really confused that morning," Perlasca remembers. "But if I had to say what it was that convinced me to stay, then I'd guess it was probably that request that I swear not to leave. Yes, because I had solemnly sworn that I would stay. And at that point, you understand, I couldn't do anything but stay."

At eleven o'clock that morning Perlasca entered the house at 33 Károly Légrády Street. "I remember that a little girl came up to me. She must have been around ten years old, and she said, 'If you save my mother I'll come to bed with you.' I slapped her. Then a group of people came over and stood around me, including the mother, and she asked me what had happened. I told her. Then, I remember, I said, 'Signora, if all the girls acted like that what could I do?' And the tension relaxed a little."

He went back to that same house a few hours later because the police had arrived with an evacuation order. A number of Spanish protectees were already standing on the porch, their bags in hand. Perlasca ran up to the fifth floor, where an officer informed him he had received orders to proceed with the evacuation. "That's not possible!" Perlasca protested. "I've just spoken with Major Tarpataky, who has given me his formal assurance of continued protection for the Spanish houses. There must be a mistake." The protest was effective, the tenants were allowed to move back into the house.

But the same scene was repeated at 25, in the other "Spanish house" on the street. Perlasca ran back to the park and found Tarpataky together with two "Arrow Cross" commanders. There he understood what had happened. The Minister of Internal Affairs had ordered the immediate evacuation of the Spanish houses because he had heard about Sanz Briz's departure and had interpreted it as the official interruption of diplomatic relations between Hungary and Spain.

Right there, in the middle of the park, is where Perlasca made his decision. He began to protest. "Hold everything! You're making a mistake. Sanz Briz has not fled, he has simply gone to Bern in order to communicate more easily with Madrid, seeing as it's no longer possible to communicate from here. You're making a very serious mistake. Go ask at the Ministry of Foreign Affairs! Sanz Briz informed two officials there of his departure. His trip involves a most important diplomatic mission!"

Then, almost without noticing what he was saying, he exclaimed, with the utmost self-confidence, "Please inform yourselves at the Ministry of Foreign Affairs! Sanz Briz left a specific note naming me as his replacement during his absence! You are speaking with the official representative of Spain!" It worked. Ten minutes later, one of the Arrow Cross commanders who had gone to telephone the ministries, came back announcing that he had orders that the evacuation of the Spanish safe houses was to be suspended "for a few days."

Perlasca got back to the embassy about one o'clock, in a state of agitation. Everyone there was depressed and upset about Sanz Briz's departure. Perlasca went into a room with Madame Tournè and Attorney Farkas and told them what had happened. "I lied. I know. All I'm asking is that you go along with me on this. Let me go ahead." Madame Tournè shook her head. She was very dubious. For her, a violation of the law in an office where she had been working for so many years was something very serious. But Attorney Farkas, Perlasca recalls, reacted differently. "I'll never forget this. He put his hand on my shoulder and said, 'That's fine. Let's get to work.'"

Attorney Farkas thus became Perlasca's diplomatic advisor. They made some important decisions right away. First of all, they had to deny that Sanz Briz had abandoned his post and that Sweden had been charged with protection of Spanish interests. They immediately called Daniellson, who said he agreed with them. Then Farkas and Perlasca sat down to compile an inventory of what was left. They had stationery, rubber stamps, blank passports. . . . Sanz Briz had left everything. There were also 25,000 pengö, a fund for war refugees. "We'll give this to Gera," Farkas and Perlasca agreed. That afternoon Perlasca took the money with him and went to see the leader of the Arrow Cross Party. He handed the money over with a hint of disdain while stating that he had come to clear up some misunderstandings that were going around about the Spanish legation. Perlasca explained the reasons behind Sanz Briz's sudden departure, and Gera, persuaded in no small part by the large sum of money he had been handed, demonstrated a great deal of understanding. As he showed Perlasca to the door he congratulated him on his advancement in his diplomatic career.

The next morning, Farkas and Perlasca went to the Ministry of Foreign Affairs to present their credentials. There was some risk that Sanz Briz may have left some public trace of his flight, but luckily he had done no such thing. Another risk was that someone might recognize the new Spanish representative as that Italian man who, until a year or so ago, had been in the meat export business. But that didn't happen either. That afternoon, Hungarian radio announced that Sanz Briz had left Hungary for a brief period and that, until his return, Spain's affairs would be handled by the embassy secretary. "That worked out well," Farkas commented. "They didn't mention your name. It's better that way."

VI
The Diary of Jorge Perlasca

But did you really walk around the streets of Budapest followed
by a police officer carrying a Spanish flag?

Perlasca laughs. "Yes, that happened too, after the last of our
cars went out of commission. I felt like some medieval war-
rior . . . but there's no question that carrying the flag was useful.
It was very useful. . . . When I think back on those times, it seems
almost unbelievable that we were able to do what we did. What it
all came down to was a great capacity for making up stories. The
Arrow Cross men wanted to cover themselves by obtaining official recognition from some neutral power, and I let on that that
might be possible. And it turned out okay. . . . Naturally, if they
had caught on to me I wouldn't be here to tell about it. But, believe me, back then there wasn't even enough time to be afraid.
There were too many things to do."

Giorgio "Jorge" Perlasca directed the Spanish legation from
December 1, 1944, to January 16, 1945, the day the Red Army
occupied that part of Budapest. Only a few people knew that he
was an imposter, and those who did know kept the secret. On
several occasions he risked his own safety, and on others, when
he presented himself as a diplomat at official meetings, he faced
the possibility that he would be recognized. If that had happened
his destiny would have been dark indeed. He made it. Many

years after the war, historians with access to official archives found a series of alarmed diplomatic notes from the period that were sent between Budapest, Berlin, and Madrid. The notes asked what Spain was up to, what was the meaning of the thousands of letters of protection that the Spanish legation was handing out to Hungarian Jews. Questions that remained unanswered. "Madrid didn't know anything about it," Perlasca recalls. "Luckily, communication was impossible. Even the smallest signal would have been enough for them to find me out."

During those days, as in the preceding months, Giorgio Perlasca kept a diary. He made daily notes about what happened to him, which he later put in order at the request of Jenö Lévai, a Jewish Hungarian official to whom we owe the first reconstruction of the extermination carried out in Hungary. What follows are the entries from Perlasca's diary about what happened to him and what he saw between December 2, 1944 and January 13, 1945.

Saturday, December 2

New raids this morning. They rounded up everybody who didn't have a Spanish safe conduct letter. I succeeded, though, in getting them all into our houses on the promise that, by the end of the day, I would have issued each of them one of our letters of protection.

I'm nervous about the fact that, unbeknownst to me, new people are being admitted to the houses. For this reason I called a meeting of the committees of all the houses and reminded them that, for security reasons, nobody was to be admitted without permission from the embassy. That's the only way we'll be able to preserve our credibility with the authorities. I think they understood.

In the afternoon, a phone call from the Foreign Ministry. They're complaining because one of their staff members who had been assigned to regularize diplomatic relations between the two countries had not been appropriately received in Madrid. Farkas told them that I would go to the ministry tomorrow to discuss what had happened.

In the evening, Farkas and I went through all the documents in the embassy and put together a plan for tomorrow. Let's hope it works.

Sunday, December 3

Total success! At noon I was received by the Vice Foreign Minister. I was a little nervous because I was afraid I might see someone who had known me from before I began passing as Spanish. Luckily, all of those staff people are in hiding, either in Sopron or in the various embassies.

The Vice Minister began by launching accusations, saying that the reason for Sanz Briz's departure wasn't clear and protesting because their representative had not been received properly in Madrid. All these things led him to deduce that Spain had no intention of regularizing its relations with Hungary. "Don't be surprised, then, if the Hungarians take retaliatory measures," he said. I told him that Sanz Briz had had to leave for Switzerland, but that the embassy was still open and that I had taken over his responsibilities. I reiterated that Sanz Briz had informed the ministry about his departure ahead of time, and that the news had even been broadcast on Hungarian radio.

I added that I did not understand the presence of their representative in Madrid, given that a week ago the ministry had requested that our embassy issue the "exequatur" (a consular permission) for a different person, Colonel Gergely. So why should they have expected the Spanish government to take seriously some unknown person who went around claiming to represent the Hungarian government?

Then I moved on right away to talk about our protectees. I reminded him that there are thousands of Hungarian citizens living peacefully in Spain, but if, for any reason whatsoever, the Spanish embassy and the Hungarian government were to fail to reach a satisfactory solution concerning conditions for the Jews under Spanish protection, then the Spanish government, albeit with great regret, would have to put its relations with Hungary under review. The Vice Minister asked me if he was to consider this a threat. Yes, I answered, with a laugh, and quickly added that, after all, our requests were not of such importance for Hungary as to require such a lengthy discussion.

At that point, the Vice Minister excused himself and left the room for a quarter of an hour. While he was out of the room, Farkas scolded me because, according to him, a diplomat doesn't use language like I had used. I tried to calm him down and assured him that everything would turn out for the best. And I was right! The Vice Minister came back with greetings from Minister Gábor Kemény and assured me that, as far as they were concerned, a way to an agreement would surely be found. I thanked him and repeated our requests. We thus reached an understanding that was also put in writing. It contains the declaration that the Hungarians are satisfied with the explanation given for Sanz Briz's departure, and obligates all units of the Hungarian military to respect the letters of protection issued by the Spanish embassy. For the Spanish side, we commit ourselves to issue the "exequatur" for their representative in Madrid, and to guarantee that our houses will grant refuge only to those Jews who are unarmed and in possession of Spanish papers. The police are authorized to check the houses but only in the presence of a representative of the embassy.

Monday, December 4

I met with Foreign Minister Gábor Kemény who introduced me to a new staff member, a Dr. Czir. From now on he will be in charge of Spanish and Portuguese affairs. He seemed to me to be a well-intentioned career officer. I pointed out to them that, given the delicacy of the request, it would take at least fifteen days for Madrid to grant the "exequatur."

In the afternoon I met with Gera. He confirmed that the Foreign Minister, the Minister of Internal Affairs, the police, and the party had approved yesterday's agreement.

I don't understand why the Hungarians want, at all costs, to send a representative to Madrid. The way I see it, with the enemy only sixty kilometers from the capital, they've got other things to think about.

Sunday, December 10

Dr. Czir confirmed, in a very determined way, what I have always thought would never happen: The Hungarian government wants to negotiate with the Western allies. Szálasi thinks that he can win them over and count on them for support against the Russians. That's why they're so interested in having regular relations with Spain! They hope that Madrid can be their intermediary! Now I have three elements working in my favor:

1) Gera's good will toward me and toward Spain.

2) The Arrow Cross's desire to establish relations, by way of Madrid, with the British and Americans.

3) The Arrow Cross's secret hope that, in the event of a total collapse, they will be granted refuge in Spain.

If everything remains as is, all I have to do is wait for the Russians to arrive. So, when they asked me at the Foreign Ministry if I thought the Allies would defend Hungary, I told them that I was convinced they would. If they had asked me to, I would have sworn to it. I would have sworn to anything in the interest of accomplishing what I've set out to do.

Monday, December 11

The improved atmosphere has made it possible for me to increase the number of people under our protection. Thousands of Jews are living in the most unthinkable hiding places. Arrow Cross groups go searching for them and when they find them, they shoot them on sight. That's why I'm trying to get as many of them as possible into our houses.

Tuesday, December 12

Some people at the embassy, either out of fear or self-interest, don't look well on the fact that I'm increasing the number of our protectees. Certainly, even the people at the embassy are living in conditions of great insecurity. What's more, Farkas and I speak very little about our problems and often all we say to each other is that everything's going fine, so the others think there are problems even when there aren't any. Good Madame Tournè considers herself responsible for the embassy's operations. She can't bring herself to understand how Madrid could abandon the Budapest legation to its own devices. She doesn't understand that it's better for us if Madrid forgets that it even has an embassy in Budapest, instead of trying to remind them of it.

Wednesday, December 13

These protectees are like children! They don't learn their lesson even when it means physical and spiritual pain. There's always somebody among them who wants to walk around the city without wearing the yellow star, or to go out when it's prohibited for Jews. They think it doesn't matter because there's always Perlasca who'll go pick them up, maybe with a couple of broken ribs. There's a certain Attorney Barta whom we've had to go get four times! Luckily, our agreements have been working rather well, the police even brought me back two people from the border. But these incidents happen continually. I think the situation could get out of control if the Russians don't get here soon.

Thursday, December 14

Protecting the Jews would be a lot more effective if those in charge of it were more conscientious, more responsible, and less egotistical.

Even before Sanz Briz's departure, a coordinating committee had been organized by the embassies of the neutral countries. The headquarters is in a villa on Rose Hill that was donated to us by the owner, an aristocrat. At the meetings the committee members were represented by Hungarian citizens. After a few meetings I arrived at the sure conclusion that their sole purpose was to create political alibis for certain people. Bottles of Tokay or cognac made the rounds and there were a lot of lovely speeches. Now that they could be really useful not one of those people is to be found.

Generally, I have good relationships with the other embassies, but not with the Swedes. We're never able to communicate with Daniellson, or with his secretaries. Every time we call there we get the same answer: either they're not in, or they're extremely busy. The only free moment they've had was when Sanz Briz was leaving and they came to the embassy to get the Swiss francs they had left here on deposit. I have a very strong feeling of disdain for Daniellson. The way I see it, a diplomat should conduct himself like a soldier, he just can't shirk his duty in moments like these. Naturally, none of this applies to Wallenberg. The Swiss, it seems to me, are doing a good job; Fehler and Dr. Zucher are good people. As far as the Papal Nuncio is concerned, I've got no complaints; Monsignor Rotta does everything he can to help.

Friday, December 15

I went to see Dr. Czir. By now I can go see him even without advance notice. I saw the Fascist chargé d'affaires, Graziani, sitting together in the waiting room with Chancellor Menci, who used to know me well. I made up an excuse and left immediately.

Saturday, December 16

To better defend our protectees I've decided to let myself be seen as often as possible. We've decided to try to visit the houses twice a day and to spend a little time in each one. To attract attention, I drive around in the embassy's Ford with a Spanish flag flying. I always take some little gifts for the police officers on duty and chat with them. It works. The police gave me an elegant walking stick with an artistic handle, the head of a Negro carved in ebony.

Sunday, December 17

Today in Gera's office I met the Minister of Internal Affairs, Gábor Vajna. Until now I've always avoided him because I prefer to deal with the Foreign Ministry. I seem to remember, in fact, that Vajna had come to Kékes when I was interned there and I'm afraid he might recognize me. But luckily that didn't happen.

Vajna is very optimistic. He thinks there won't be any changes before spring and that the Russians, at least for some time, will be kept back from the area around Budapest.

But he asked me again when the Hungarian representative could leave for Madrid. I gave him an evasive answer.

When I was alone with Gera, I asked him how it could be that the same Hungarian government that had refused the Horthy armistice was now looking to obtain another one? Gera replied that the October 15th double-cross had been the work of the Jews, that it was an attempt to do something behind the Germans' backs. I asked him why he thought the Germans would now allow the Hungarians to conduct their own separate negotiations? Gera answered that the Germans knew the Hungarians' intentions and didn't want to pose any obstacles. Is it possible that the Germans want to take advantage of the Allies' sympathy for Hungary? Are they hoping, perhaps, that after the negotiations have begun, they'll be able to participate as well?

Monday, December 18

Today I went to the Foreign Ministry to communicate that the Spanish government had sent a telegram reiterating its positive opinion concerning the Hungarian request but that, given the delicacy of the international situation, it is forced to ask the Hungarians to be patient. I assured him, however, that the Spanish government will certainly be in a position to respond favorably by December 31. Dr. Czir (by now the officer in charge of the Foreign Ministry in Budapest because the higher ranking officers are almost always in Sopron) responded that everything was going fine. That surprised me quite a bit. Suppose he's right? What will become of my organization if the Russians don't get here before the winter's out? I hope I'll be able to keep faking it.

Tuesday, December 19

The situation of the Jewish children is increasingly serious. There are a lot of orphans whose parents have been deported and who are also homeless. Both the Swedes and the Red Cross have set up welcoming centers. There are also some parents who, although they're living in the safe houses, prefer, for security reasons, to have the children stay in these new centers.

Up to now the Spanish embassy has taken in five hundred children. Now we've learned that the Arrow Cross authorities intend to transport all orphans into Budapest. I don't understand what they want to do, but some of their officials say that they've decided to exterminate them. They want to deport them to Germany. They're mad! Even before they got there, at least half of them would be dead.

Wednesday, December 20

I had a difficult discussion with Gera. He tried to explain to me that Budapest had to be freed of its superfluous inhabitants. I was able to get from him, however, that none of the children will be deported; they'll be brought into the big ghetto. This is a circumscribed area in the center of the city whose streets have been barricaded against attempts to get out. Some 60,000 Jews are living there, without gas or electricity, and most of them are children or sick people. Everyday, five hundred of them die from hunger or illness. I go there often to try and bring out relatives of our protectees. I'm delivering medicine and food to hospitals that do not respect the most elementary rules of hygiene.

Friday, December 22

On the initiative of the Papal Nuncio there was a meeting today, at the Portuguese legation, of neutral country representatives. Weyermann, the new Red Cross representative, was there too. We decided to draft a common diplomatic note.

Saturday, December 23

Eight o'clock in the morning, at the Nuncio for the final draft of the note.

Fehler, the Swiss delegate, was asleep on the table as we talked. Daniellson didn't come and Wallenberg tried unsuccessfully to find him. Only the Nuncio decided to wait for the Swedish minister, the rest of us signed and left.

After the signing, I asked to see Monsignor Rotta in private. I told him the whole truth. At the beginning he refused to believe it, but then he enjoyed hearing how I had succeeded in tricking the Germans. He was happy to hear that I was a Lombard like him. He told me that in the interest of the common good my deceit could be forgiven, but he advised me very strongly not to say anything to his secretary, Monsignor Verolino. He said he was so old fashioned and anxious that he wouldn't be able to sleep at night if he knew.

I don't know what will happen if the Russians are delayed much longer. The Arrow Cross is expecting to receive approval from Madrid for their representative and in Madrid, naturally, no one knows anything about their request. So it's impossible that any approval will be forthcoming. If they should find me out, I could always ask for refuge from the Papal Nuncio or the Swiss legation. But in that event, I can see nothing but tragedy for our protectees.

Here is the text of the diplomatic note which we issued today:

> The undersigned, representatives of the neutral powers accredited in Budapest, have already courteously appealed to the Royal Hungarian government on two occasions, asking it to intervene on behalf of the Jews who are being persecuted and treated as outlaws. Now that the Royal Government has decided that it is necessary to close off the Jews in a ghetto – and in this note we will not discuss the reasons for this decision – the representatives of the neutral powers intend to take a further diplomatic step so that children, at least, will be excluded from this measure. It would be totally incomprehensible to punish the innocent, just as it would be to speak in terms of legitimate self-defense with respect to these absolutely harmless beings. Even if the measure were to be carried out for the purpose of preventing possible disorders, it would remain no less unacceptable to punish children for that reason. There are those who say that the Jews are the enemies of Hungary, but the norms of law and conscience are enough in themselves, even in time of war, to condemn all actions taken

against innocent children. Why is it necessary to force these children to live in a place that resembles a prison and where they will be able to see only the misery and suffering of women and old men, persecuted solely on the basis of their racial origin. Every civilized people respects children, and the entire world would be terribly surprised if it were to learn that Hungary, a country with a noble and Christian tradition, has taken action against minors. The representatives of the neutral powers hope that the Royal Government will wish to look favorably upon this request and allow all children (together with the mothers of those who are still nursing) to be moved outside of the ghetto to protected places made available by the diplomatic delegations, or to centers set up by the International Red Cross. Together with the acceptance of this request, which has solely humanitarian objectives, it will be necessary to take care that the people selected to provide assistance to the children are politically beyond reproach and capable of providing a patriotic education.

Budapest, 24 December 1944
Angelo Rotta, Apostolic Nuncio
Carl Ivan Daniellson, Swedish minister
Harold Fehler, Swiss representative
Jorge Perlasca, Spanish representative
Conte Pongràcz, Portuguese representative

Sunday, December 24

The day began badly. This morning none of the cars would start and the rack wouldn't work either. I felt like I was closed off in the Villa Széchenyi. By telephone I received the news that some Arrow Cross men had forced their way into the Swedish embassy and arrested the staff. I immediately called the Foreign Ministry to protest. I also called the police.

Around ten o'clock, an Italian, Santelli, lent me his car and at last I was able to move. At the embassy everything was quiet. In the city, all the bars and stores are open, although they have few goods to sell. I went looking for a Christmas tree for Madame Tournè.

At the embassy I met with a high ranking Arrow Cross who told me that the military situation has gotten very serious but that the city will be defended. I replied that that would mean thousands of people killed and the destruction of one of the most beautiful cities in Europe. He agreed, but he said that the Germans were determined to resist. I asked myself how long this insanity can go on.

Later, as I was on my way to the Apostolic Nuncio to exchange Christmas greetings, I ran into a group of young people, surrounded by Nazis and Nyilas armed with machine guns, marching toward Pest. I asked the head of the group what their intentions were. He told me they were taking the youngsters to the ghetto. It was an excruciating scene. There must have been more than a hundred youngsters who had been walking for more than an hour in the twenty degree cold. They were exhausted. Some of them would fall and struggle quickly back on their feet. All of them were crying.

I hurried immediately to the Nuncio and asked Monsignor Rotta to come with me to the Foreign Ministry. Rotta didn't agree; he said that after the raid on the Swedish embassy there wasn't anything else to be done. I proposed to threaten the Hungarians with an interruption of diplomatic relations, but he told me he couldn't do that without first consulting with the Vatican.

I found this intolerable. I insulted the diplomats and walked out. In my hurry, I forgot to kiss his ring.

The scene at the Foreign Ministry was really strange. All the offices were open and there wasn't a soul in the building. Finally, I found the concierge who told me that the offices were empty because it was Christmas. But I could feel that there was something else in the air. I started to hope that Budapest might be declared an open city.

I went around to visit the houses and deliver some Christmas presents. Madame Tournè bought some food, and prepared some bags and boxes, along with a small amount of money to distribute to the neediest. But the embassy is running out of money, so I often add some of my own.

Back at the villa, I was finally able to get something to eat about four in the afternoon. At five I heard some shooting from automatic weapons and mortars. Half an hour later it was all quiet again.

The refugees have prepared the big Christmas dinner. A big Christmas tree stands out in the hallway. That evening, I went into town for a social engagement.

The people who had invited me to dinner live at 10 Ferenc Liszt Square. After dinner I took a walk over to 72 Emperor Vilmos Street to the apartment that Dr. Friedrich had left me in the beginning of November. On the way, they stopped me twice on the street and treated me roughly. There were Arrow Cross and Nazis. I ran into a police officer and asked him to escort me home. On the way home he told me that he had it from absolutely reliable sources that the Russians had cut off the road to Vienna and that within hours the city might be surrounded. He told me that the Russians had crossed the Danube north of the city and then had suddenly headed for Budapest. This strategy of theirs hadn't been expected and they were able to gain a sixty kilometer head start and were now on the outskirts of the city. Now I understand why I hadn't been able to find anybody in the entire Foreign Ministry!

Monday, December 25

The Germans have closed the bridges over the Danube, a sign that the war is now close to the city. Luckily the Buick is parked at the embassy. You can hear shooting and the streets are deserted. We were expecting a truck with food rations but it hasn't come. The food situation is starting to get precarious.

I went around to all the houses and gave them all the following speech:

"Signori, until now the Spanish embassy has been able to defend you, but now I consider it my duty to inform you that the hastening of events will make your protection less secure. The city is surrounded, Nazism is living its last hours, there is no more authority, and I still don't know who I can turn to in case of violence. And I am afraid that there will be a lot of violence in the city. It may happen that the extremists, at the last moment, will join together with the criminal element, and attack the Jews. A month ago I asked you to put away your arms. Now I am asking you to keep them ready. In case of attack, defend yourselves!"

They are all very frightened. Many of them are looking for new, safer refuges. I tried to dissuade them from doing so.

Around ten o'clock I told Farkas that I was going to see what was happening at the villa, because no one was answering the phone there. Despite the general protest, Farkas wanted to come with me. At the Chain Bridge the Germans stopped us. I informed them that I was a Spanish official and that I was going to my home. The officer made a phone call and let us go. At the beginning of Istenhegyi Street we were stopped by Hungarian soldiers. Their commander told us that we could proceed under our own responsibility. Finally, on foot and running, we reached the villa. The refugees were expecting me, the table was set.

When I left, I didn't take any of my personal effects so as not to frighten them. I left my clothes, files, and valuables in my room. When they asked me if I would be coming back the next day, I didn't know what to answer.

We came back early to Pest. It looks like the Germans are serious about defending the city. There are bands of Nyilas going around killing "traitors" and sacking the city. Around five o'clock one of these bands stopped us in Mussolini Square. "Spanish embassy," I told them, but according to their leader that wasn't enough. I had to show them my passport and my diplomatic identity card. But our idiotic driver also gave him Farkas's passport, and when he saw that the attorney had a Hungarian last name and spoke Hungarian, he was infuriated and, playing with his pistol, tried to make him get out of the car. He called him "dirty Jew" and it looked like he was going to kill him. Luckily, an army officer came over and we were able to return to the embassy. I told Farkas not to leave the building again.

While I was out, a colonel of the military police came to the embassy to inform us that the Hungarian military command in the area wants to ensure the tranquility of the legation and prevent any madmen from doing anything like what had happened to the Swedes. The refugees are very worried, they think it's a trap, and they begged me to refuse the offer of help. But I see it from another point of view, and since the Nuncio has accepted the military police's offer of assistance, I don't see why I shouldn't too.

Tuesday, December 26

All night long you could hear the sound of airplanes flying over the city.

In the morning I went with Farkas to the area command. I had to take him with me because often the soldiers don't speak any foreign languages. We spoke with a colonel. He told us that there are bands of Arrow Cross sacking the city and that they have joined up with common criminals to commit atrocities. The military police want to protect us from these raids.

I accepted a group of four guards armed with bombs and machine guns and I asked them to keep an eye on the house opposite the embassy, in Podmaniczky Street, which serves as our annex. The officer agreed. Around noon the four military police arrived, armed to the teeth, but dressed in civilian clothes. This aroused my suspicion so I went back again to see the colonel. In great confidence he told me that a group of officers had gotten together and decided to take the highest possible number of military police away from the Germans in order to have enough troops available to maintain order when the Russians arrived. The guards had been deployed in such a way as to keep them from entering into contact with our protectees.

Wednesday, December 27

The food is running out. I have an agreement with a baker to bring us bread every day. I bought some ham from the Red Cross and we purchased dried fruit, sugar, honey, lard and anything else we could find on the black market. We take this food to the safe houses.

The people there are getting more and more nervous. They're holed up in the bathrooms, in the halls, and on the stairways. A lot of people are unable to get into the houses. Their faces are wrought with fear, terrible to look at.

In the afternoon the military policemen's commanding officer called to tell me that, by order of his superiors, they will accompany me on the streets. When I go on foot they will walk behind me, at a distance of two steps, carrying the Spanish flag. When I go by car, they will sit in the back seat. Excellent!

Thursday, December 28

I looked for Vajna, the Minister of Internal Affairs, but I couldn't find him. When I got to the Hotel Esplanade, near the Margarita bridge, I noticed that a group of civilians and soldiers were hurrying out of the building and heading toward Kálmán Széll Square. They told me the Russians were coming. I heard some shots and explosions, but I couldn't understand where they were coming from. A soldier pointed to a group of people who were running about a hundred meters away from us. They were Russians.

We turned the car around and went off in the opposite direction but in Kálmán Széll Square we found ourselves in a combat zone. We had already started thinking about leaving the car there when we found a quiet street and were able to get away from the area where the shooting was taking place.

I heard that the chief of police had set himself up in the basement of the City Hall. I went over there and talked with Colonel Gyula Sédey, a police commander. He gave me a good impression. He said he was sorry about what the capital and the people were going through. I told him that the city was in the hands of bloodthirsty madmen and that the streets were full of the bodies of their victims, many of whom were women and children. He pointed out that the personnel available to him are not sufficient to reestablish order. At that point, I mentioned that there were at least two thousand police there in the building, but he answered that he didn't want to spread them out around the city because it wouldn't have done any good. And so he keeps them all there nearby to avoid the worst.

In the safe houses life goes on in silence. Aside from the dangers of the war and the scarcity of food, security here may be better than before. Tarpataky has deployed a good number of guards around the "international ghetto."

The building at 5 Phoenix Street was hit by a bomb. Two people were killed, others were wounded. Another bomb at 33 Károly Légrády Street. Here too, two dead and a number of wounded. The house in Podmaniczky Street was also hit, and a bomb exploded on the balcony of the embassy. Fortunately, no one was hurt.

Friday, December 29

At dawn three more military police came to the embassy. Now there are seven. Our protectees are frightened again and I am worried too. So much so that I refused to take in Professor D'Alessandro and his fiancée, who wanted to move over here from the Italian Cultural Institute which has been hit several times by bombs. Since he's very well known to the Germans and I know that they're looking for him, I was afraid that by taking him in I would be setting up a trap for him. I found them a place to stay with the International Red Cross.

Saturday, December 30

Last night a terrible thing happened. They took a group of Jews from the ghetto and slaughtered them in Ferenc Liszt Square and in Eötvös Street. First we heard the screams and imploring cries of hundreds of people, and then we heard the shots.

At dawn I went to the scene and saw that the victims were for the most part women and children. In the morning, I went to the Hotel Hungary to meet with the representative of the International Red Cross, Hans Weyermann. All of a sudden, a Hungarian officer came up to me and asked me to come with him to the banks of the Danube. My guards tried to send him away, fearing an assassination attempt. Then they settled for standing there beside me with their machine guns pointed at the officer.

The whole river bank was covered with snow, but in front

of the Café Hungary and Café Negresco the snow had turned blood red. You could see hundreds of dead bodies that the water hadn't carried away because there were blocks of ice in the river. These people had been murdered during the night and then thrown in the water.

I told the officer that I had seen a similar thing near the Margarita bridge and asked him why he had invited me here. His aim was to convince foreigners that the army had nothing to do with these things. That's true, I replied, but the army is charged with seeing that the law is respected and protecting the rights of citizens, not with standing by and watching atrocities like these. They told me that the victims had been forced to walk for about two kilometers, in double file, with their hands tied, without shoes and socks, and completely naked. Then they made them kneel down on the river bank and shot them in the back of the head.

The officer handed a woman over to me who had saved herself by falling in the water before the shots. They had pulled her out of the water and were rubbing her down with camphor. I took her back to the embassy with me.

Sunday, December 31

This morning my life was saved by pure chance. At eight o'clock I got in the car to go visit our houses. We had food and medicine. As we were leaving, I heard them calling me to go and answer a phone call. To save time, I gave the order to leave without me. I would join them for the next trip. Somogyi was driving the car, then there was the official from the Red Cross and the usual two military police. In Pannoia Street the car was machine gunned by a Russian aircraft. Somogyi was wounded in both ears, though not seriously, but the military policeman who was sitting in my seat was killed instantly. We've lost our last car. From now on the food will have to be delivered by hand.

It's New Year's Eve and we spent the evening in high spirits. Madame Tournè offered us some Spanish wines from the embassy reserve, and even our protectees were able for a few hours to forget everything that was happening around them.

Even the gunfire was muffled, like fireworks to welcome the new year. For the first time in a week we can't hear bombs exploding or the sound of aircraft. There is only silence.

Tuesday, January 2, 1945

The first two days of the year have gone by amid dangers and minor incidents. Today the director of our house on Rose Hill called. They informed me that the Russians had entered the refuge and that the children were now safe. There was a Russian officer who spoke German and I told him that from then on it was up to the Soviet army to protect the children.

At the embassy we're almost out of food. We had bread and squash for lunch and the same for dinner. Fortunately, my friends in Ferenc Liszt Square invite me over to eat. Outside the temperature has gone down to fourteen degrees. In three months I've lost thirty-seven pounds.

Wednesday, January 3

The telephone doesn't work anymore. Today they sounded the alarm. I heard that the military command wants to transfer the Jews from the international ghetto to the one in town. I'm worried, it seems unbelievable to me that the command should send out its troops on a task that is practically superfluous. And then, in the ghetto, there's no room for another 15,000 people.

In the afternoon I met with Tarpataky. He hasn't received any orders but, in his opinion, now that everything has been lost, we can expect some sort of vendetta from Vajna, something ugly. He has been asked to move over to Buda but he hasn't done it. He's barricaded inside a bank in Emperor Vilmos Street.

Thursday, January 4

Young Bardos came to the embassy at dawn to tell me that they were evacuating his house. I started running and I met up with a column of Jews being moved from the safe houses to the ghetto. Someone said they were taking them all there and then they were going to set the ghetto on fire. Some police officers told me the same thing.

I went on a quick tour of the ghetto. Thousands of dead bodies lay on the streets. I went to see Sédey, but he told me that there was nothing he could do. I spoke with Ferenczy's aide-de-camp and with another officer who works as a liaison between the Foreign Ministry and the area command. They all confirm that the order has come from the Germans.

Along the way, I was witness to various incidents between the Nyilas and the military police. The Nyilas round up Jews and beat them up, and those who can't walk are shot between the legs. The military police oppose the violence and they even pick up the packages left behind by the weakest of the victims.

I haven't been able to put myself in contact with the other embassies. My guards have also confirmed that the Germans want to incinerate the ghetto. The Spanish houses, for the moment, won't be touched.

Friday, January 5

Young Bardos came back at five-thirty. He said that the Arrow Cross have gone back to rounding people up. I went with Farkas to see Tarpataky. I let him know that I want to talk to Minister Vajna. He gave me a written order according to which the raids are to be temporarily suspended for the houses protected by the embassies.

Accompanied by a police officer I went around the area showing the contents of the order. The police officers were all satisfied, but the Arrow Cross were not.

The news about the possible incineration of the ghetto got to the houses before I did. By the time I arrived, there had already been a lot of suicides. In the house in St. Stephen's Square a woman had thrown herself off the fourth floor. In the other Spanish houses the men had decided to use their arms. If I were certain that we had enough available weapons I myself would give the order to attack. I think that the police force might even fight on our side.

As I walked along the street, people came up to me and expressed their gratitude. The military policemen were visibly proud to accompany a person who was so respected.

An officer from the Portuguese legation came to the embassy. He asks that we take over the protection of the Portuguese houses because the Portuguese honorary consul, Count Pongrácz, has taken ill and is no longer able to carry out his duties. He told me that five hundred Portuguese protectees are about to be transferred to the ghetto. I promised him to take care of their protectees but I asked for a formal request on the part of Count Pongrácz. In reality, the gentleman hasn't shown his face since Christmas, but not because of illness. Because of fear.

Saturday, January 6

I went to the Portuguese houses. Unfortunately the Jews had already been taken away at dawn.

I ran to see Vajna. By now it's difficult even to reach the City Hall; the rain of bombs and grenades is getting thicker and thicker. Bombs have fallen in the courtyard of City Hall; the Russians must have found out that the command headquarters are there. But the bombing is useless because the headquarters are under the building in a massive labyrinth that can withstand even the most powerful bombs.

Underground I found Wallenberg and Zurcher of the Swiss embassy. They had also come to ask Vajna to suspend the transfer of their protectees to the city ghetto. I asked them to let me speak first, because I was convinced that as a Spaniard I had a better chance of convincing that madman. They agreed.

Ernö Vajna, Minister of Internal Affairs. It's unbelievable how a man who appears to be so distinguished and jovial can be in reality such a wicked soul. We talked for two hours. The whole thing was very trying because Vajna's German is worse than mine. I told him right away that the time had come to surrender, that further resistance made no sense and would only cause more death and the destruction of the city. I told him that an immediate capitulation would obligate the victors to show greater comprehension and that it would make it possible to put a stop to the bands sacking the city. I tried, for a long time, to make him understand that by now the war was lost, and that what was happening was senseless and shameful. I told him that the world will not easily forget it. I appealed to his patriotism and I reiterated that, together with the other diplomatic representatives, I was ready to do whatever I could to facilitate the process of surrender.

Vajna replied that he refused to talk about surrender. According to him, the city must be defended to the last man. He says that a German column from Esztergom is about to arrive in Buda.

So I changed the subject. According to Vajna, the Jews are dangerous outside of the ghetto because they could sabotage the resistance. I told him that was impossible because they were all disarmed. There is no more room in the ghetto, there's no water, gas, food or medicine, there are thousands of unburied dead. If a warm wind should start to blow there will be a danger of epidemics. I also told him that the German command had declared that it did not want to interfere and that, therefore, the responsibility for what happened was his alone. I told him that burning down the ghetto with seventy thousand people inside would be an evil deed that the world would never forgive. His answer was, "You know the wickedness of the Jews." I told him I didn't want to continue talking about that and, as far as I was concerned, the evil had a completely different source.

After a two-hour discussion, Vajna had conceded only that the Jews protected by our embassy would be settled outside the ghetto, but still in the immediate neighborhood. I told him that wasn't enough. I gathered up my courage and delivered the following speech:

'Signor Vajna, in my last letter I stated clearly that the Spanish government will be forced to take retaliatory measures if our protectees should become victims of your cruel treatment. If, by January 10, the Spanish government has not received a reassuring communication from me, the retaliation will begin. You should know that there are three thousand Hungarian citizens living in Spain and that the government has decided to intern them and confiscate their property, in the event its protectees here in Budapest are mistreated. The same measure is ready to be applied to all those Hungarians who wish to go to Paraguay and for whom one hundred and fifty provisional passports have been issued here in Budapest.' (All of this was a colossal bluff. I believe there are no more than three hundred Hungarians in Spain.)

Vajna responded that I had spoken in a tone unworthy of a diplomat. I told him the situation demanded it. He then asked me what guarantees I could give him that Hungarian citizens in Spain would not be disturbed. I answered, 'Signor Vajna, the Latin people have never persecuted foreigners without reason. If you agree with my requests, which are legitimate and humanitarian, I don't see why the governments of Spain and Paraguay should bother your countrymen!'

The ferocious beast grew calm. I had the impression that he was beginning to understand what the consequences of his actions could be. He remained thoughtful for a moment and then he said, in an emotional voice, 'Hungary is going through the greatest tragedy in its history.' I answered, 'You can do something to alleviate it! If you love your country, you must act reasonably!'

He gave in. He assured me that the Spanish protectees would not be harmed. And that he would have the news broadcast on the radio. At that point, I told him that Wallenberg and Zurcher were waiting outside and that I would not consider myself satisfied unless he offered them the same assurances. I even invited him to accompany me on a tour around the city, so that he could get a better idea of what was really happening. He was amazed at this request.

At the end of our talk he was a broken man. I went out and briefly informed Wallenberg of the result.

Sunday, January 7

Vajna's assistant came to get the telegram that I was supposed to send to Madrid. I said it had to be transmitted by military radio because no other service was working. Farkas and I felt lost. What will the Spanish government do when it receives the telegram? Will it declare that it no longer has a representative in Budapest? In the end, we decided to go ahead and send the telegram, but to have it go by way of Bern. Let's hope Sanz Briz understands. In the message we said that everything here is fine and that, thanks to the cooperation of the local authorities, all of the protectees are well. We also forwarded the request of the Hungarian authorities concerning the protection of Hungarian citizens in Spain and Paraguay. Let's hope the answer doesn't come too soon.

Today the military police assigned to our protection were recalled, including the two that accompanied me in my movements around the city.

Monday, January 8

I wrote to Colonel Sédey requesting new guards. He immediately sent me a police inspector and another officer. I noted that the transfers of Jews had been suspended and that police sentinels had been stationed at various points in the ghetto. It looks like Vajna is keeping his promises.

You don't hear any more shooting in the area around the ghetto. There's a strange silence.

Tuesday, January 9

They just informed me today that young Bardos has been missing for three days. I am enraged. Bardos was picked up in the area near Mussolini Square. They tell me he was killed right away. He's a very brave young man and very humane.

Wednesday, January 10

I went back again to City Hall. There are fewer and fewer people there and they're all depressed. I couldn't find Vajna or Sédey. I have the impression they've been given the order to disappear. Tarpataky is still barricaded inside his little fortress.

Saturday, January 13

Everything's in order in our houses, under the circumstances, but there's no more food and the people are afraid of the bombing. The House in St. Stephen's Square has been hit twice, although no one was hurt. By now it's almost impossible to walk in the area. As of this afternoon I'm no longer able to leave the embassy because even Eötvös Street has become a combat zone. Some Hungarian soldiers came by with news of the other houses. This evening the fighting stopped and everything is quiet.

VII

Basements, Coal, and a
Telephone Number
on Her Arm

A Monsieur Georges Perlasca,
Budapest

*Aujourd'hui, le 16 janvier 1945, au moment où les
troupes sovietiques sont penetrés dans notre quartier et
que nous nous sentons enfin liberées de la tyrannie nazie,
nous sentons le devoir de vous remercier de tout ce que
vous avez fait pour nous, en nous soutrayant d'une morte
certaine. Nous n'avons jamais douté de votre courage, de
votre abnegation et des risques que vous aviez encourrus
pour nous en toute occasion. Nous tenons à faire cette declaration solennellement.*

*Nous soussignés, en vous gardant une eternelle recon-
naissance, signons la presente declaration.*
Budapest, le 16 janvier 1945

Today, the 16th of January 1945, as the Soviet troops
are entering our neighborhood and we finally feel liberated from Nazi tyranny, we feel the duty to thank you for
all that you have done for us, saving us from certain death.
We have never doubted your courage, your self-sacrifice,

and the risks which you have incurred for us on every occasion. We solemnly wish to make this declaration.

We the undersigned, in eternal recognition of your efforts on our behalf, sign the present declaration.

Budapest, January 16th, 1945

The paper is decades old. A white sheet of paper with no letterhead. The "solemn declaration" is typewritten without much concern for accents or spelling. Under the date, in a single column, are the names of sixteen people. Next to the names are their signatures, written with a fountain pen. They are the names of the people who, for forty-eight days during the siege of Budapest, kept the Spanish legation open and functioning, in the absence of its director, all the while issuing thousands of free safe conduct letters, and finding food and money to protect the throngs of Jews who had come to the embassy searching for a way to avoid deportation.

"Aujourd'hui, le 16 Janvier 1945, au moment où le troupes sovietiques sont penetrées dans notre quartier. . . ." They didn't wait for an official declaration of the city's liberation before drafting their testimonial to Perlasca, in the middle of all the emotion and tears. They waited only for the shooting and explosions to stop and to hear the voices of the Soviet soldiers speaking to them through their megaphones. Many of the Jews of Pest remember those voices which reached them in their hiding places in the basements of their houses. "Don't give up." "We're on our way." Then the long silence. And finally, for those who had the courage to be the first to look outside, the sight of the Soviet tanks rolling through the streets.

That's also how things went at the embassy in Eötvös Street, where the fighting continued right up to the end. The proposal to draft the testimonial immediately was made by Attorney Zoltán Farkas, one of the few who knew that Perlasca was not in fact the chargé d'affaires, was not even a Spanish diplomat, that he was only an Italian lost in the middle of the war, and the driving force behind a grand enterprise. Attorney Farkas must have guessed that the certificate, in the uncertain aftermath of the war, would be useful to the Italian; help him get back home, or at least to establish his identity. He had been Giorgio, then Jorge, and now he had become Georges.

"Poor Attorney Zoltán Farkas," Perlasca recalls, "We had become friends. He must have been sixty years old, a tall, well-built man who had been decorated in the First War and was married to a noblewoman from Vienna. He liked fighting for something and taking risks. Throughout that entire month, his eyes shone as if he had become young again. Now I'll tell you how he died. On the evening of the day they wrote the letter, some grenades exploded, killing some Russian soldiers. The Russians came into our headquarters, convinced that the attack had come from there. Almost all of them were drunk. They beat people up and took all their watches. They found a bunch of automatic pistols under a pile of coal and were convinced they had discovered a snipers' nest. They went wild and started beating everybody up and threatening them with hanging. Farkas stood up to them and tried to explain that what they'd found was a collection of pistols that belonged to a Spanish minister, and which, as anyone could easily see, had never been used. He got extremely upset and then ran upstairs and out onto the roof, together with two police officers. Then Farkas, probably because of the emotion and his lack of agility, fell off the roof to his death."

January 1945 was a bitter cold month in Budapest. Long stretches of the Danube were frozen over and the great Chain Bridge, struck right in the middle by a bomb, was cut in half. The streets were full of snow and dead bodies. The German army and the Nyilas put up a fierce resistance which was marked, right up to the end, by the activity of uncontrollable armed bands. For days, the Soviet troops had to limit themselves to defending the positions they had established during their initial attack on the city.

On the morning of January 18, a Soviet tank opened a breach in the wooden wall surrounding the Dohány Street synagogue and the small neighborhood of narrow streets behind it, and rolled into the ghetto. The first soldiers through the wall saw no human beings on the streets. The whole place looked empty. They kept moving forward until they noticed that the park around the synagogue, the offices of the Jewish community, and some stores and warehouses were filled with frozen corpses. It was only after several hours, and even then very cautiously, that living people began to emerge from the houses and the basements. Tens of thousands of them, mostly women, children, and old people: The ghetto of Budapest, horribly ravaged by the fighting, had survived.

On the same day, liberation came for another twenty thousand Jews who were closed up inside the "international ghetto" in the neighborhood around St. Stephen's Park. But another twenty days would pass before the hill of Buda would be liberated. The city filled up with lines of weakened and exhausted Jews, trying to find out news of their families and relatives, looking to see if their own houses were still there, or trying to find something to eat. But nothing was known yet about what had happened to the young adult men, the tens of thousands deported to the work camps to dig for copper in the Bor mine, or to build the underground shelters and trenches that were supposed to defend Vienna. It wasn't for another month that the first groups of these men began to make their way back into the city.

The liberation of Budapest was not a joyful event. On the contrary, there was quite a bit of ill feeling. The Hungarian families that had occupied the houses of the Jews or taken over their stores did not, for the most part, want to give them back. They exhibited documents with official stamps certifying their rights, ready to resort to force to defend their new possessions. The same people who had stood on the streets watching in indifferent silence as the columns of deportees were taken out of the city, now adopted the same attitude toward the returning survivors; those emaciated, silent men with their shaved heads, paralyzed by the memory of what had been done to them or what they had seen in the camps, and alienated even more by not knowing what had become of their families. Many former members of the Nyilas bands, including some well-known people, now presented themselves to the victors, claiming to be sympathizers and even asking to become members of the Communist Party.

The new Soviet military government managed the post-liberation with a hard and suspicious hand. Tens of thousands of Jews, waiting for permission to return to their homes, were parked in camps, assisted by the International Red Cross. The diplomatic delegations which had promised to save twenty thousand Jews in the "protected houses" of the "international ghetto" were treated with the coolness reserved for neutral parties. The envoy of the King of Sweden, Raoul Wallenberg, vanished completely. Nobody knew what had happened to him. Giorgio Perlasca, the Italian businessman with a Spanish diplomatic passport that identified him as Jorge and some testimonial certificates that identified him as Georges, certainly did not have the right credentials to be embraced as a brother by the victors. With some difficulty, he succeeded in reaching a command of the Red Army, only after he had been shot at by a couple of drunken Cossacks. He presented himself to the commanding officer who immediately put him to work digging up dead bodies that were buried under the ice and snow in the streets of Budapest. He managed to escape from this forced labor and again took shelter with friends in the capital.

"I had a total of 3,700 pengö with me, a leather bag, a kilo of spaghetti, a few walnuts, and two packs of cigarettes," Perlasca recalls. "Everything I owned had been stolen from me by the Russians at the legation or had been destroyed in the fire at Villa

Szécheny. The adventure had come to an end, but another one was beginning; the adventure of hunger."

There were a lot of people who knew about what he had done. Perlasca gave a copy of his notes to Jenö Lévai, a former officer in the Austro-Hungarian army, to whom we are indebted for much of the existing documentation of the persecution of the Jews in Hungary, a work of great patience compiled from witnesses' accounts and documents that managed to survive the destruction provoked by the siege.

Perlasca's presence and his activity were recognized in a host of certificates, full of official stamps and signatures, just like the ones he had signed as the bogus consul. The acting Executive Committee of the Hungarian Jewish Association recognized his work immediately:

> We take great pleasure in certifying that, during the Szálasi government, you helped us on many occasions and that, in those days, you risked everything to help the Jews through your contacts and your own personal efforts. In those hard and critical times, you were always at the side of those people who found themselves in serious difficulty, and now we are happy that the moment has come in which we can express our gratitude for your constant commitment and for your noble human sentiments. According to our information, your activity on behalf of Israelite Jewish citizens made it possible for several thousand of them to save their lives and overcome the period of the siege of Budapest as well as the well-known political difficulties.

In the beginning of March 1945, representatives of the new government drafted a document for Perlasca which was to be essential for his safe conduct. This one too was different, though not all that much, from those that he and Farkas had issued:

> To all public authorities and private parties:
> The assembly of the 4th District of the Social Democratic Party certifies that, during the preceding regime,

Signor Giorgio Perlasca, undertook superhuman efforts on behalf of the oppressed and the persecuted. As the person charged with supervision of the safe houses, he intervened at all times, often at the risk of his own life, to help the people under his protection. His luminous demonstration of philanthropic and humanitarian spirit merits the most profound expression of our affection and gratitude.

Perlasca recalls, "They wrote out that certificate in the same building where I used to go to recover our protectees who had been arrested – the very same rooms. And unfortunately, it happened that I was able to recognize people that I had seen there before, dressed in other uniforms. I had gone there to try to do something on behalf of Tarpataky, to testify that he had always conducted himself as a gentleman. I think that's the only time I've ever presented myself as an Italian anti-fascist."

By May the war was over, the Third Reich had fallen. In the midst of the wreckage Europe's trains and railway stations started working again. On May 29, 1945, a brief notice in the Budapest daily announced the departure from the Hungarian capital of an Italian friend. At the East station, as he waited for the train, a small crowd gathered to wish him good-bye, friends and people whose lives he had saved. A delegation of the residents of the house at 35 St. Stephen's Square assembled on the platform and presented Perlasca with his last certificate:

> We are sorry to learn that you are leaving Hungary, in the direction of your native land, Italy. On this occasion we wish to express to you the affection and gratitude of the several thousand Jews who survived, thanks to your protection. There are no words to praise the tenderness with which you fed us and with which you cared for the old and the sick. You gave us courage when we were on the verge of desperation and your name will never be missing from our prayers. May Almighty God reward you.

The next day, the Budapest daily *Kis Ujsag* carried an account of the departure. Waiting for the train, the reporter had walked around the station together with Perlasca. "All around us is the usual panorama: groups of men, broken and exhausted, walk by us. Near Baross Square, the smoke is so strong it catches in our throats. Children play happily in the reserve water tank which they call the 'swimming pool.' Perlasca looks very thin and pale, only his eyes are shining."

Giorgio Perlasca had a long way to go on his way back home. He passed through Bucharest and then Sophia. From there he went to Istanbul, where he got on a ship that took him to Naples.

Hungary, as part of the agreements signed at Yalta, was handed over to Stalin and became a "People's Republic," which rebelled against the USSR in 1956 and was punished by an invasion of tanks sent from Moscow. After returning to the Soviet bloc, she was granted a bit more autonomy than the other member countries, so much so that she earned the nickname "the most comfortable barracks in the prison camp." In 1988, when a brief notice in the newspaper led to the rediscovery of the "self-proclaimed Spanish consul," the country was already on the eve of the great change and, in 1989, when the witnesses who still remembered the "Just Man" told their stories to the press, the change was well under way. The remains of Imre Nagy, the Communist who had led the rebellion against Moscow in 1956, were disinterred from an unmarked grave and reburied in an imposing official ceremony. Thousands of Germans from the Democratic Republic escaped from their enclosure by coming down through Czechoslovakia and into Hungary, which allowed them to cross over into Austria. They were then parked in huge camps where they slept in their Trabant cars. Twice a week the Moscow-Tel Aviv shuttle made a stop at the Budapest airport. Thousands of Jews were leaving the USSR. To the south, Ceausescu's Romanian regime fell suddenly and the Hungarians cheered for the return to freedom of their "separated brothers" from Transylvania.

January 1990. We're in Budapest with a small television crew filming a program on the Perlasca story. We track down witnesses and film the locations. We make friends – above all in the ghetto. We go often to Dohány Street, the site of the Temple. The biggest synagogue in Europe has remained externally intact. Every time we go by it, we meet an old man, a street person. Each time he looks at us with his eyes wide-open and starts talking to us, in English: "This is ghetto. Do you understand?" Then he points to his chest. "Me . . . your guide." On the other side of the iron fence you can see the grounds, with the graves. From a few angles you can see the inside; it's in very bad shape. We hear that there's a project to restore it, financed by a certain Emanuel Foundation, whose president and main contributor lives in the United States. The Foundation's patron is the actor Tony Curtis, who arrived in New York with the name Bernard Schwartz, the son of a Jewish family that had escaped from Hungary in the twenties. They tell us that Tony Curtis came back to Budapest a little while ago, to great applause, and that he knows how to express himself quite well in Hungarian.

Behind the Temple, the Jewish quarter shows only rare signs of rehabilitation. A small store sells Bibles, vestments and miniscule books, an inch and one-half wide: *Jewish Holy Days*, *The Encyclopedia of Jewish Nobel Prize Winners*, *A Dictionary of Famous Jewish Musicians*. The apartment buildings, as in many other popular neighborhoods in Pest, are atrium houses, built around a cement courtyard with a tree planted in the middle. The courtyard is also used for beating rugs and carpets. Many front gates are decorated with the Star of David or the seven-branched candelabra, the menorah.

We walk around carrying our television camera, setting up and taking down the tripod, making a lot of noise, but nobody shows any curiosity. In one courtyard, however, an old woman carrying two big shopping bags stops to talk. She smiles. "When I was young I worked in show business too. I also acted in the cinema."

"What part did you play?" I ask.

"The Yiddish mother."

We have a list of witnesses who knew Perlasca but some of them say they don't want to appear on television. They are shy about being seen. Others, however, are willing to speak in front of the camera and to go back and visit the places where things happened.

We make an appointment with Mrs. Hoppi Palmer, an employee in the offices of the Jewish Community of Budapest. She takes us to one of the Spanish safe houses where she had hidden in 1944 and where she had seen Perlasca. She has never been back there since. Mrs. Palmer goes down the steps to the basement of the house which, back then, was situated at 44 Pannonia Street. She starts to have trouble breathing. Then she starts to cry. "Everything is just the way I remembered it." She points to a corner of the room.

"There was a pile of coal over there," she says. "Every time the Nyilas came near the house, we children were put there under the coal. Bombs fell nearby. In front of the house there was an empty space where the Germans set up an anti-aircraft gun. People said that if you had to choose between the bombs and the Nyilas it was better to be killed by a bomb." She points to another corner. "My mother used to sit there and near her was an opera singer. Whenever the desperation or the fear was too great, the singer would start singing arias or marches, and she calmed everybody down that way. Perlasca came to bring food. Mr. Gaston Tournè also came by quite often. If it hadn't been for them, we would never have survived. We would have ended up being killed on the banks of the Danube."

Mrs. Anna Konigsberg teaches music in a middle school in the Ferencvaros neighborhood. We ask her if we can come see her at school to speak with her and her students. She asks us, visibly worried, whether that's really necessary. "No, no, it would be better not to. The principal wouldn't really appreciate it, and

Ferencvaros isn't a neighborhood where Jews are liked very much."

So we go instead to the entryway of the building in St. Stephen's Square. Several people stop to ask what's going on, why is that woman being interviewed. We explain to them what we're doing, and they walk away without making any comment.

Mrs. Konigsberg was eleven years old back then, but she remembers that after the war the adults talked about "this Signor Perlasca." "They'd say, 'It's thanks to Signor Perlasca that we're still alive.' They didn't know who he was; they said he was an ambassador, and that the fate of the world depended on him. . . . But in the People's Republic you didn't talk about these heroes in public. Only a little, about Wallenberg and the mystery of his disappearance."

You didn't talk. Or you talked only with people you knew well. After the war, the anti-Semitic laws were repealed, but no damages were paid for the material losses that people suffered. The Jews of Budapest got into the business of buying food produced in the countryside and selling it in the neighborhoods around the synagogue. But it didn't last more than a few years. The new regime launched a "campaign against black marketeers," identifying them with the Jews.

The new Communist government allowed the Jewish religion, but people who went to temple were looked on with suspicion . . . just as Jewish schools, although formally allowed to operate, were frowned upon.

Newspapers began publishing articles about how the "Jews are trying to capitalize on their suffering, as if they were the only ones who suffered." People who had been awarded possession of Jewish homes confiscated by the pro-Nazi government were now allowed to keep them by law. In official administrative documents they were indicated as "Good Faith Possessors." In 1946 there were even pogroms against the Jews who had survived.

And so those who had undergone forced labor or had survived

the concentration camps quickly began to replace the term "Jew" with "ex-deportee," "member of the obligatory work service" or "former racial persecutee." Year after year, the situation convinced everyone to stop talking about the "catastrophe" and maybe even to forget about it. High up on Gellert Hill, in Buda, a great victory statue was erected: a female figure forty-five feet high, holding an olive branch in her arms. The woman looks toward the east, the direction the Red Army had come from. In 1948, Raoul Wallenberg, whose fate was still a mystery, was nominated for the Nobel Peace Prize, a candidacy supported by Albert Einstein. In Budapest, funds were raised to build a monument to him in St. Stephen's Park: a bronze statue, twenty feet high, of St. George doing battle against a snake whose head was engraved with a swastika. But when inauguration day arrived, it was discovered that the bronze figures had been stolen, dragged away by a team of plow horses driven by Soviet soldiers. Several years later, the figures were rediscovered, in Debrecen, in the entryway of a penicillin factory. St. George was now fighting in the name of science against the Koch bacillus.

"Ábrahám Rónai, a survivor who was twelve years old in 1944, was asked three years later to play in a film about what had happened.

"Do you remember *Valahol Európában* [*It Happened in Europe*]?" he asks. "It was a famous film, written by Béla Balázs, the great film scholar. It was the story of a gang of kids just after the end of the war. I was one of the gang."

Today Rónai is sixty years old and still working as an actor. He emigrated to Israel in the late 1940s, and he was one of the principal architects of the "discovery" of Perlasca. He's a massive man with a shaved head.

> [T]he reason why in films and in the theater they've often asked me to play the part of the Nazi. But, when I was twelve years old I was really a good-looking kid. A kid who was already acting in the theater, a 100 percent as-

similated Jew. I was a student at the King Mathias Junior High School, where we wore the national uniform, and when they ordered us to wear the yellow star, I thought it looked good on the blue uniform jacket. My family was wealthy. My father was a producer of corks for wine bottles, and he had a company with some businessmen from Seville who supplied him with cork. My father was taken away and deported to the mine in Bor, so I became the head of the family. When they said that the ghetto was going to be closed down by the end of November, I put on my uniform and ran to the Spanish embassy. There was a huge doorman there who didn't want to let me in. I climbed up on him and kept saying to him, "Don't you have any kids? Can't you show a little pity?" In the end, he let me go in, and I handed in photos of my mother, my sister and my father too. That's where I saw Perlasca. I remember we spoke in German. He said I should take my family to a house that today is at 22 Balzac Street.

Ábrahám Rónai doesn't remember all this with sadness or anger. He forces himself to remember it with happiness.

There was a gang of us kids in that house, and we had permission to go outside two hours a day. One day, a blond boy with blue eyes came into the house, dressed in the uniform of the young Nazis. He gave me his hat and the sash and belt from his uniform and asked us if we wanted to do something useful for the Jews still in the ghetto. He was a member of the Zionist youth organization. Myself and a couple of other kids, dressed in those pieces of the uniform, would leave the house and go stand in front of the stores where people would stand in line for something to eat. The only thing you could get was Vitaprix. Do you know what Vitaprix is? A jar of tomato and green pepper concentrate, one of the few things that you could find to eat back then. Our assignment was to stand in front of the stores and attack the people who came out with food. We'd yell "dirty Jew" at them and push them around until we got their jars of Vitaprix. After that we'd run to the ghetto and get inside by giving the Nazi salute. Then we'd throw the jars of Vitaprix into the basements where our people were dying of starvation.

Rónai saw Perlasca again on Christmas Eve of 1944.

> The Nyilas had broken into the house and taken away a bunch of people, including my mother and my sister. Perlasca arrived – I thought he was the ambassador's secretary. He was accompanied by a group of Hungarian police officers. One of them carried the Spanish flag. He started shouting orders in German while, together with the police officers, he threw the Nyilas out of the building. He yelled, "This kind of behavior is inadmissible in a fascist state! You're going to pay for this!" He managed to get everybody back in the house. The next day it was Christmas. The director of the house was a Christian, a very good person. He invited all the children to eat Christmas dinner at his house.
>
> Then there were two weeks of fighting. We were all hiding down in the basement. At dawn on January 17, they knocked on the door. Who is it? It was a Jew from the house across the street; he told us his name. We looked at him standing there in front of us, with his yellow star still on. He told us, "Don't you know? We're free. For two hours now, we've been free." We went outside, and I saw this Cossack carrying a machine gun. I walked over to him, but he sent me away.
>
> A week later we went back home. We couldn't even stand up anymore from hunger, and we were all full of lice. We couldn't do anything except lie down all day. I asked my mother for her shoes, and she gave them to me. I went outside, and a Russian soldier gave me his beret. Dressed like that I started hitching rides from the Russian trucks and went out into the country to look for food. I came to a little village where they fed me for three days. I walked back home, and my father was there. He had managed to escape from Bor, but he had to take a long route home, through Romania.

"But Mr. Ábrahám Rónai, after it was all over, did you ever

try to find Perlasca again?" I ask. The old actor has been expecting this question and he knows what the truth is: He had forgotten. He raises his hands with a great laugh and then begins to pound his chest: *"Mea culpa, mea culpa, mea maxima culpa ..."*

With Rónai we go to get something to eat in a restaurant behind the synagogue where they cook the best goose in all of Budapest, not too far from the *Little Canteen* bar, where the melancholy Rezso Seres composed the famous song "Gloomy Sunday." He became immensely rich on the royalties, but his song acquired an infamous reputation. It was said that it drove people to suicide; that whoever listened to it was seized by an irresistible urge to jump out the window.

We meet a woman who, unlike Rónai, had tried to find Perlasca, but had then decided that she didn't want to see him again. Mrs. Weisz, clerical worker and English translator, together with her family, was protected in the house in Pannonia Street, and she too gives us her testimony while standing in the entryway of the building, surrounded by disgruntled tenants whose access to the elevator has been blocked for a few minutes. Mrs. Weisz has brought some photographs with her from when she was a young girl. One of them shows her in an elegant white tennis outfit, racket in hand and a short pleated skirt. In the picture she stands in an odd, oblique position, with her head tilted. Forty years later, she tilts her head the same way.

> Perlasca came to see me several times and I remember him for his kindness. Little things and big things. He was a help to all of us because it was the first time we saw someone who took us by the hand without asking for anything, in times when our homeland had become our own worst enemy. Our neighbors, our classmates, the people that we had grown up with and lived with, had become enemies. Seeing Perlasca was a wonderful experience for me, enough for a whole lifetime. A human being who, in circumstances like those, maintained his humanity and lent

himself to help people he didn't even know and whom nobody defended. I saw him the last time at the end of the
siege, when he came to the house to say good-bye. He said
that it wouldn't be possible for him to come again because
by that time the city had been divided in two, and he
wouldn't be able to move around, but that anyway we
wouldn't need him anymore. The fighting would be over
in just a few days, and he was sure that we would make it.
Then he disappeared, and I didn't hear about him again until the notice was published in the newspaper. He came to
Budapest, but I didn't want to go see him. I prefer to keep
the memory of how I saw him in this entryway and of how
he said good-bye to us. I'm not exaggerating when I say
that he is the only hero I've ever met, and I want to preserve that memory just as it is. I hope I will always be able
to remember him like that. I wish him a long and healthy
life.

When she finishes talking and is finally free of the micro-
phone, Mrs. Weisz thanks everybody and excuses herself with
the tenants of the building for the bother created by that brief occupation of the entryway. Then she walks out alone onto the long
avenue that used to be Pannonia Street.

In January 1990, Hungary is on its way to having its first free
elections. Forty-five political parties have entered the race, but it
is really a two-party contest. The Liberals, an urban party based
in Budapest, propose themselves as the champions of modernity
and a cosmopolitan Europe. The Democratic Forum – Catholic,
Magyar, with most of its support in rural areas – speaks in favor
of tradition and the idea of the nation. The campaign speeches
are about the privatization of the state-owned industries, repara-
tions to be paid to those whose property had been expropriated
by nationalization, purging the public administration of Communist bureaucrats. But before long, the campaign begins to
turn ugly. Leaders of the Forum start attacking the Liberals and
label the party as "the party of the Jews." There is talk again of

their "disproportionate influence" in public life and in the professions. A demonstration is organized under the windows of the headquarters of the public television to protest because too many of the journalists are Jews. People start pulling out statistics about proportional representation again. The "Jewish question" is back.

There are no Italian books dedicated to the persecution of the Hungarian Jews, but it was nice to discover a very thin book by Giorgio and Nicola Pressburger, a collection of ten short stories entitled *Homage to the Eighth District*. It begins like this: "The tourist who plans to visit Budapest, royal city of an empire that ceased to exist more than half a century ago but still famous for the gay life of its upper crust and for the multiplicity of the peoples that it has welcomed, will happen into the Eighth District only by mistake . . ."

What follows are the stories of Franja, Nathan, Uncle Gustave, Rachel, first in the Eighth District, as the home of the poor Jews was called before the war, and then, on the same streets, after the "catastrophe."

Giorgio and Nicola Pressburger, twin brothers, were born in Bratislava in 1937. Their family moved to Budapest and there, in 1944, the children survived the siege. They got out of Hungary after the 1956 rebellion. Thirty years later they transcribed their childhood memories and published them in the book. Nicola, an economic journalist, died in 1986. Giorgio, after a successful career as a theater and television director, is now a well-known writer.

I meet with Giorgio Pressburger, who has heard a lot about Perlasca and seen the television program about him. He tells me how, when he saw the TV images of the front of the building in St. Stephen's Square, he had a sudden flash of memory, a kind of *déja vu* experience.

> I don't even know myself if it's true, but suddenly I saw myself again in that house. I was seven years old. I slept there for two nights, I think. I have this vision of a base-

ment; I remember a laundry room. We had been picked up
and taken to the race track to await, as I learned later, our
turn to be deported. But my mother had a safe-conduct letter, issued by the King of Sweden. I think it must have been
a forged document. She showed it to a guard, and they took
us away from the race track. I remember that we walked
for a long time, and I was carrying a heavy bag full of jars
of marmalade that our mother had taken with her when she
left the house. That feeling of fatigue has remained with
me my whole life. I've dreamt often of going swimming
with my brother, only he is in front and I'm behind being
dragged to the bottom. I think about it every time I'm in a
train station carrying a bag. And I still have the habit, every
time I go on a trip, of taking a really heavy bag with me.
My whole life, I've been carrying heavy bags while I wait
for trains.

We ask Giorgio Pressburger about Vitaprix, and he remembers it well. And he also knows about Tony Curtis, alias Mr.
Schwartz, and about "Gloomy Sunday," which he starts to whis-
tle. He confirms that in Hungary no one talks about the Holocaust in public anymore. A "tacit agreement."

In Budapest, we ask our Hungarian guides to help us find Paul
Street. It still exists, and the Botanical Garden and the courtyards
with little sawmills described in the book still exist too. But there
are no signs or other tourist information to help you find it. It's in
the Eighth District, a short little street with rundown buildings.
There are no gangs of young children around, and the only gath-
ering place, the *borozo*, is a little wine bar in the basement of one
of the buildings. In the early afternoon it starts filling up with
hundreds of old men who come to drink white wine and seltzer
to wash down their lard and onion sandwiches. In the *borozo* you
drink standing up, leaning on the counter. A lot of the men have
those bulbous red noses typical of alcoholics, and a lot of their
lungs have been destroyed by tuberculosis. All of them have
fond memories of Molnár's book, especially the little blond,

Ernö Nemecsek, who gets out of bed to participate in the battle and dies of pneumonia. But they don't have much else to say about it. What else can they say? So much history has gone by since then. So much ugly history that saw neighbors from the same building become enemies and fight each other. Would it make any sense today to argue in the courtyards about who was right and who was wrong? No, you can't do that.

Budapest is a city with a lot of places that evoke too many memories and encourage silence. In one of them, not far from Paul Street, a piece of history that people wanted to forget went on for years, in the form of an odor that wouldn't go away. It's the block where the Italian Cultural Institute was located. The Institute was damaged in the war and used, in 1945, as an infirmary for Italian soldiers released from German prison camps. When they left, the place was disinfected with phenol found in the Germans' military supply dumps. The chemical compound most certainly killed all the bacteria, but it also permeated the entire Institute. It seeped into the books and the furniture and spread into other buildings on the street. Even ten years after the war was over, it was a place where passersby still smelled the stench of the war and lengthened their stride.

If the city is frightened of its memories, there is even less talk of the past in the country, the vast flat Hungarian countryside where urban dwellers pass through but never stop. To the west are the plains of Pannonia, beyond which, on the other side of the narrow strip of Yugoslavia, lies the Adriatic and the port cities of Fiume and Trieste. And to the east the endlessly flat universe of the puszta followed by the Carpathian mountains and finally, the steppes of Asia, home of Attila, whom we think of as the symbol of human cruelty but whose name Hungarians are quite happy to give to their children.

People from Budapest traveled east only when necessary, to buy horses, for example, as Perlasca did. Army officers were sent there for punishment. Travelers returned with stories of strange foods and customs and a world divided between frightening castles and isolated villages, whose inhabitants seemed "slow, calm, perhaps already dead, but very intelligent."

In the 1930s, the Budapest government decided to send out an expedition to the east composed of parliamentarians, writers, artists and agronomists. They came back with stories of absolute poverty and strange customs and superstitions, just like the stories told by the English aristocrats who traveled to eastern Hungary in the eighteenth century and who had been shocked by their bizarre encounters with the local population. One Englishman told of a visit to the city of Hermanstadt, among ruins of castles built by the Knights Templar and the remains of Roman fortresses, where he was the guest of a noble family who taught their children ancient Greek poetry, and where he was awakened one night in an inn by a man ranting, in perfect Latin, about the divine qualities of schnapps: "*Schnapps, Domine, est res maxime necessaria omnibus homnibus omni mane.*"

In one of the local shops he saw a portrait of a certain Walter Skote, identified as "the most famous man in all of Europe." Another English traveler had a similar encounter during the same period. He told of how he had stopped, in the plains of Transylvania, at a "Juden Knipe," the pejorative term used for an inn run by a Jew. A young boy he met there asked him if Walter Scott were still alive, and was very unhappy to learn of his death. He pulled out a tattered copy of the German translation of *Ivanhoe* from his jacket pocket and explained that he and his coreligionists considered it to be a novel of Jewish liberation because right alongside the Saxon and Norman knights rode Isaac of York and the beautiful Rebecca.

Those lands in eastern Hungary were to remain separate from, and yet somehow linked to, the rest of the world, in and out of time, moving back and forth for decades between Hungary and Romania, Poland and Russia, until history finally caught up with them. It was sudden, systematic, fast and brutal. Between March and July 1944, in the area east of the river Tisza, the SS deported or killed 440,000 Jews, as well as a very high but imprecise number of gypsies, Jehovah's Witnesses, followers of the Church of the Seventh Day Adventists, and political dissenters of all kinds.

Jews had been living in that area for centuries and, as the Nazi Reich began to expand, the local population was joined by Jewish refugees from Slovakia and Poland. Even up to the beginning of 1944, every city and town had its Jewish community with its Hasidim, its scholars who studied the Talmud and the Kabbala, and its Yiddish newspapers.

In March 1944, the little town of Maramarosziget, now on the border between Hungary and Romania, became part of Zone I of the German "dejudification" program. A sixteen-year-old boy, Elie Wiesel, survived the concentration camps and wrote about his experience. In his work, *Night*, he tells how the first deportations began in 1942 and how people in the town justified them as necessary to the war effort. But then it happened that one of the deportees came back into town; Moshe the Shammes a young servant at the Hasidic synagogue, was "poor, insignificant and invisible." He told how everybody had been killed and that only he had survived because, as he lay there wounded, the Germans had taken him for dead. But the people didn't listen to him. In 1944, the Germans arrived in the town. Jews were denied the right to possess gold, jewels, objects of value. Everything had to be turned over to the authorities under pain of death. Then decrees were handed down prohibiting Jews from entering restaurants or cafés, from traveling by train, from going to the synagogue, from leaving their houses after six o'clock in the evening. Then the requirement to wear the yellow star. Wiesel's father, an important man in the Jewish community, tried not to rub salt in the wounds: "The yellow star? So what? It can't kill you."

Then they closed the Jews into two ghettos. "They appointed a Jewish Council, a work committee, a social services office, a department of hygiene. It was just like a regular government bureaucracy," Wiesel wrote. "A regular government bureaucracy." Everything seemed fine, but Moshe the Shammes said, "I warned you."

One night they took everybody away. According to the statistics, some 12,000 Jews from Maramarosziget were killed. And Maramarosziget is so small you can hardly find it on the map, and if, by chance, anyone happened to go there, they wouldn't notice a thing. Many years after the war, Wiesel went back to his home town. There was nobody left from his family, but when he pushed open the wooden front gate of his house, he heard the same creaking sound that he heard as a kid.

And what about Bilke? Bilke wasn't far from Maramarosziget, but it was even smaller and less well-known. It's in the mountains, surrounded by thick forests, with six mountain streams running through it; 7,000 inhabitants, 1,000 of whom were Jews. There was no electricity, and the only telephones in the town were in the police station and the post office. On May 24, 1944, the Jews were all taken to Auschwitz.

Among them was an eighteen-year-old girl named Lili Jacob. She survived Auschwitz, and in the last months of the war she was transferred to another camp, in Dora, near Nordhausen, in Germany, where she was liberated by the American army. On the day she was liberated, the camp's SS officers fled, and the prisoners took over their lodgings. In one of their lockers Lili found, together with some clothes, a photo album in a blue cloth binding. She began leafing through it and recognized some familiar faces. Then she saw a picture of herself. They were pictures of the Jews of Bilke, taken upon their arrival at Auschwitz by a German soldier and given as a present to his "dear friend Heinz."

Lili Jacob took the album home with her. Two years later, in exchange for ten thousand corona, she gave permission for copies of the photos to be made by the Jewish Council of Prague. Lili used the money to pay for tickets for herself and her husband, Max Zelmonovic, and they emigrated to the United States.

They arrived in New York at the end of 1948, and from there

they went on to Miami. Max got a job as a butcher, and Lili worked as a waitress at a restaurant called Famous. One day they saw a notice in the paper for an apartment for rent. They went to see it and discovered that the owners were Jewish too. Max stayed for a while to talk about the rent and the terms and conditions of the lease. The owners told him they were inclined to give them the apartment because they had made a good impression. Then, assuming a confidential tone, the landlady said to Max, "But your wife seems a little strange to me. . . . Is she absentminded? Why did she write her telephone number on her arm?"

The incident left Lili upset and disheartened. Ten years later, in 1958, she got the chance she'd been waiting for. During the winter season, Miami was host to the popular radio show "Queen for a Day." Aimed at a female audience, the show gave women the opportunity to make their dreams come true. Contestants were selected for a competition that was decided by the studio audience, using an applausometer. Several times in a row Lili failed to get through the selection process, but then she was selected with four other contestants. She said, "Every time I glance at my left arm and see that tattoo I remember the horrible time that I spent in a concentration camp. I wish that tattoo could be removed." She won the applause contest and was crowned queen. Fifteen days later a surgeon removed those numbers from her arm.

Twenty-two years later, her photo album turned out to be an extraordinarily important historical document. Some "revisionist" historians had begun to say that the extermination of the Jews was a lie, that at Auschwitz there had never been any gas chambers or cremation ovens. But among the one hundred and eighty-nine photographs found by the girl from Bilke there were photographs of those buildings too, and you can see them perfectly. It was only when the SS decided to flee the camp that they destroyed them with dynamite.

In 1990, the new liberalized Hungary was visited by 38 million tourists. As in the other countries of Eastern Europe where freedom of speech has returned, research into the historical archives has begun. Opposition leaders have come to light; some of the dead have been rehabilitated. But rarely has the research gone farther back than 1956. The researchers only go back beyond that date after a lot of resistance, when they do it at all. With regard to the extermination of the Hungarian Jews, the only country where the Nazis failed to complete their project, the previously unknown story of Giorgio Perlasca has been just about the only "new fact" to reemerge.

VIII
The Freight Station

In September 1990, at the age of eighty, Giorgio Perlasca was invited to visit the United States as a guest of honor. In Washington and New York he was given awards, embraced by ambassadors, and interviewed by the press. His picture and his story appeared in millions of copies of Sunday supplements and magazines. A group of psychologists questioned him for hours, trying to understand what had motivated him to do what he had done.

Perlasca's new public life, the television appearances and awards ceremonies, didn't change him a bit. Asked to speak at celebratory banquets, he thanked his hosts for their hospitality, and apologized for not being an orator. He lit cigarettes in places where smoking was strictly forbidden, and always admonished his listeners not to "forget that the Eastern European gypsies were also victims of the Holocaust." And he visited the construction site which, in 1992, would become the home of the Holocaust Museum, dedicated to the memory of "evil," and located right next to the other museums and monuments that celebrate all that is "good": democracy, scientific achievement, a healthy relationship between man and nature.

He also met other saviors, both like and unlike himself. There was Mrs. Miep Gies of Amsterdam, who protected the Frank family and managed to save Anne's diary when she was deported. And Mrs. Yukiko Sugihara who, together with her husband, succeeded in bringing thousands of Polish Jews across the Soviet Union to safety. In 1940, her husband, Senpo Sugihara, was the Japanese consul in the city of Kovno, Lithuania, when crowds of Jews fleeing from the Nazi advance started showing up at the consulate asking for visas. He telegraphed Tokyo asking for instructions, and the answer came back telling him that he was forbidden to issue visas. At that point, he announced his resignation but gave himself a week's time, and in seven days, with his wife's help, he was able to issue six thousand safe transit visas, inventing the most tortuous possible routes with detours through Siberia, Mongolia and China, and final destinations as unlikely as Shanghai, Hong Kong, Singapore, and even Curaçao. The Soviets put him in a concentration camp for fourteen months, and when he finally returned to Japan he wasn't able to find a job, but he would never stop saying that "from a human point of view, I had no choice."

Every time Perlasca was asked what episode he remembered most, he always cited the "case of the twin boys."

The railroad cars would leave from the freight station in Budapest. They were freight cars with nothing in them but a layer of straw covering the floor and a garbage can for excrement. The Jews were loaded into the cars, about eighty to a car, and then the doors were sealed shut.

Before loading, the Jews would gather on the platform in a line, herded forward by the Hungarian police under the watchful eyes of the German SS. The loading operation was carried out with dispatch.

The diplomatic representatives of the neutral nations used to go to the freight station regularly to see what they could do. They were a few men trying to snatch anybody they could from the death shipment. They would stand there and call out, "Anybody who has a Swiss safe conduct letter, raise your hand." "Is there anyone here who is under the protection of the Spanish government?" "Is there anybody here who has forgotten their Swedish safe conduct papers?" It was a matter of seconds. A last-minute attempt whose outcome turned on a fleeting glance or a timely plea, a question of quick reflexes or a moment of distraction among the soldiers. It was still possible to save somebody, before the cars were sealed. The incident Perlasca remembers happened on one of those mornings.

> The line was moving forward, and I saw these two boys in the middle of it. They must have been twelve or thirteen years old, and they were identical. A couple of twins, all alone. I had the Buick from the consulate parked right there beside the platform with the Spanish flag on the fender. I really don't know why, but those two boys really struck me. They had dark complexions and curly brown hair. To me they looked like the same person, multiplied by two. As they passed in front of me, I reached out and grabbed them, pulled them out of line, and threw them into the car. I yelled out, "These two people are under the protection of the Spanish government!" A German major came over and wanted to take them back. I stepped in front of him and said, "You have no right to take them! This car is Spanish national territory. This is an international zone!" The German major pulled out his gun, and we got into a shoving match. The driver and I were holding the door closed and he was trying to pull it open. Raoul Wallenberg was standing nearby. He turned to the major and said, in a very decisive tone, "You don't realize what you're doing! You are committing an act of aggression against the territory of a neutral country! You'd better think very carefully about the consequences of your actions!"
>
> The major wouldn't give up. He started waving his pistol under my nose and said, "Give me back those two boys, you're interfering with my work." I said to him, "Is this what you call work?"
>
> Then a colonel came over to us. The major put his gun

away and explained the situation to him. I gave my explanation too. I repeated once again that the two boys were under the protection of the Spanish government and that the embassy car was an extra-territorial zone. The colonel gestured with his hand to the major, indicating that he should desist. Then he turned to me and said, very calmly, "You keep them. Their time will come. It will come for them too."

So we kept them. We'd done it. After the Germans walked away, Wallenberg said to me, under his breath, "You realize who that was, don't you?" "No," I said. "That was Eichmann."

When he thinks about that morning at the freight station, Perlasca, even today, sees those two boys standing in front of him.

I took them to one of our safe houses and once we were there, I realized that they weren't two boys after all. They were brother and sister. Now that I was able to look at them more closely I could see the differences between them. They had those little differences that begin in the development phase; the boy a little bit of hair on his upper lip, and the girl just the first signs of breasts. We kept them with us for a few days and then we handed them over to the Red Cross. I never saw them again. I don't know what finally became of them, although I think they made it. But I'll always remember when I saw them walking forward together in that line. I think I'll remember them rather than so many others because they were so strikingly alike, because they were alone, and because they were so beautiful.

Perlasca had never seen Eichmann before that morning. Wallenberg, however, knew him well. Having arrived in Budapest together with the eight German divisions that occupied Hungary in March 1944, SS Lieutenant Colonel Adolf Otto Eichmann, thirty-eight years old, commander of subsection B4 of Section 4 of the SS Head Office for Reich Security, following his experience in Poland and Slovakia, was in charge of the "final solution" for the Hungarian Jews. He set up his headquarters in the Hotel Hungary and began organizing and dealing. Between March and July 1944, he succeeded in organizing the deportation of nearly all Hungarian Jews from the provinces to the camp in Auschwitz. Now the time had come to render "*Judenrein*" (Jew free) the capital, the last of the six zones into which his organizational plan had divided Hungary. Eichmann's method was always the same: Set up a Jewish council – *Judenrat* – and give it the responsibility for working out the practical details of deportation. Wallenberg succeeded in contacting him and was able to make some deals. Very simple ones: money in exchange for Jewish lives; expatriation permits, or safe conduct letters in exchange for dollars. For the neutral diplomats, what went on each morning at the freight station was a last desperate effort to save lives. For Eichmann, on the other hand, even if two boys were able to escape their "appointed time," it wasn't all that important, because, sooner or later, their time was bound to come.

Adolf Eichmann did not leave Budapest until the very last days of the siege. He went first to Vienna and then to Berlin. After the German defeat he succeeded in escaping without leaving a trace. He was tried *in absentia* at the Nuremberg trials together with the other Nazi leaders.

In 1960, his name showed up again in newspapers all over the world. Adolf Eichmann had been captured by agents of the Mossad, the Israeli secret service, in the suburbs of Buenos Aires. He had been living in Argentina for fifteen years, under the false name of Ricardo Klement. Nine days later, Eichmann was put on a plane and flown back to Israel to be put on trial. The Argentine government protested to the United Nations about the methods adopted by the Israelis, but it was not able to block the transfer. The government of West Germany could have requested Eichmann's extradition, but it did not do so.

For six months in his jail cell in Jerusalem, Eichmann was interrogated by the investigating magistrate, Avner Less, and responded to his questions in a respectful, civil tone. He was examined by six psychologists who declared, one after the other, that he was of sound mind. On April 11, 1961, Adolf Eichmann appeared in the district court of Jerusalem, charged with fifteen crimes "having committed, together with others, crimes against the Jewish people, crimes against humanity, and war crimes during the whole period of the Nazi regime and especially during the Second World War." When he was asked how he wanted to plead, Eichmann responded, with respect to each count, "not guilty within the meaning of the indictment."[1]

The trial lasted six months. The defendant, for the first time in any trial, was present in the courtroom protected by a glass cage. He was provided with a simultaneous translation which allowed him to follow the testimony of the more than one hundred witnesses who recounted the experience of deportation and extermination. Not once did his face betray any sign of emotion, except for a tic which caused his upper lip to twitch for the duration of the trial. Eichmann was defended by Attorney Robert Servatius from Cologne, who had already represented several Nazi leaders at the Nuremberg trials. His defense strategy was rather limited. In a statement issued before the trial opened, Servatius said only that his client had performed "acts of state," "acts for which you are decorated if you win and go to the gallows if you lose."

Throughout the questioning, Eichmann declared that he had always simply obeyed the orders of his superiors. He admitted that "naturally" he had contributed to the extermination of the Jews, but that he had never killed a Jew, nor given an order to kill a Jew. He said that "naturally," if he "had not transported them, they would not have ended up in the hands of their executioners." In a final statement he said that he would have liked to "be reconciled with his former enemies."

Eichmann was found guilty on all charges and sentenced to death. The Court of Appeal confirmed the sentence. Defense Attorney Servatius then appealed to the Supreme Court, which denied the appeal on May 29, 1962. Adolf Eichmann was hanged on May 31, 1962. His body was cremated and the ashes were sprinkled on the waters of the Mediterranean Sea off the coast of Israel. It was the only death sentence ever issued by a court of the State of Israel.

The Eichmann trial was also the occasion in which the world was forced to come to terms with the reality of the Holocaust. Each witness recounted his or her personal experience as a survivor of a plan aimed at placing Europe under the thousand-year domination of Hitler's Reich, with the other peoples reduced to slavery and the Jews eliminated from the face of the earth.

Hundreds of journalists covered the trial. Among the many who wrote about it, Giovanni Cerrato, a journalist from Padua, wrote a piece for the newspaper *Il Resto del Carlino* about an Italian who had seen Eichmann up close. It was the story of Giorgio Perlasca, told with sufficient detail to arouse further curiosity about his exploits in Budapest, but the article did not provoke any reaction at all. Perlasca remembers that the only person who said anything to him about it was his landlord who said, "Bravo, Perlasca, I see you conducted yourself well during the war." Not much later, however, a strange thing happened.

One day, as Perlasca was getting ready to reenter the front gate to his apartment building, two men approached him. They asked him if the story in the newspaper was true and Perlasca said, yes, it was. Then they asked him if he would be willing to confirm his account of the episode before the court in Jerusalem because, the two gentlemen said to him, the incident he remembered would be a very important element for the defense. After all, Eichmann had allowed those two boys to go free, and that could be used as evidence of his humanitarian behavior. Perlasca recalls that the discussion, outside the front door of his house, didn't last more than ten minutes. He simply told them that wasn't the way things were, and that he certainly wasn't going to speak in defense of Eichmann. He recounted the episode in the same terms forty-five years after it happened, when he was invited to Jerusalem to receive an award:

"You're interfering with my work . . ."

"Is this what you call work?"

"Acts for which you are decorated if you win and go to the gallows if you lose."

Giorgio Perlasca and Adolf Eichmann met each other for only a few minutes one morning during the ordinary course of the macabre business of transporting Hungarian Jews to Auschwitz. It was a brief match, between a calm lieutenant colonel in the SS and an emotional Spanish diplomat. They were more or less the same age, one had power and the other did not. But the match was won by the latter, who was neither Spanish nor a diplomat.

What I like most about this episode, which has remained impressed in the memory of Giorgio Perlasca, is that a choice was made. The Italian saw the two twin boys and reacted immediately, thinking that something could still be done to save them from being murdered. The German lieutenant colonel may not even have seen them (I imagine them curled up on the seat of the car) and with a simple gesture of the hand, he let them live. For him, they weren't two people but two numbers. A statistic.

Among the famous correspondents that covered the Eichmann trial was Hannah Arendt, the former student of Heidegger and philosopher in her own right, who wrote *The Origins of Totalitarianism*. She asked *The New Yorker*, which obviously agreed, to send her to cover the trial. She wanted to see Eichmann "in flesh and blood," the man known as the architect of the "final solution", the man who had established the train schedules, the quotas of deportees, the living symbol of evil, the human being responsible for the planned assassination of five million of his fellow human beings.

Hannah Arendt observed him scrupulously for months. The son of a bus company employee in Solingen; a poor student who enlisted in the SS in the hope of finding a career which civilian life surely would not have offered him; a man fond of saying that *"Amtsprache,"* the jargon of the military bureaucracy, was the only language he knew; a man who believed in his superiors, in the hierarchical distribution of responsibility. The detailed accounts of the trial that Hannah Arendt sent back to *The New Yorker* provoked a debate that went on for years because the author criticized the prosecution's conduct of the trial, and did not allow to go unmentioned the role of passive collaboration in "the final solution" played by the Jewish Councils. Evidence about this collaboration came out at the trial. One episode concerning Hungary – with loud protests from the audience at the trial, composed at the time largely of survivors from Budapest, against those who had not given them timely information that would have allowed more people to be saved – became the occasion for deeper reflection about the behavior of the Jewish Councils generally.

But more than anything else, it was Hannah Arendt's interpretation of Eichmann himself that led to the controversy. According to Arendt, contrary to the then current view which portrayed Eichmann as an inhuman monster, the defendant in the glass cage was instead a "normal" person; he was simply "a man incapable of thought." But what was it, she asked herself, that had caused him to stop thinking?

In his most important statement at the trial, Eichmann admitted that he had known about Hitler's decision to go ahead with the physical extermination of the Jews, and declared that he had thought this was "a horrible thing, an illegal thing." He said that the sight of dead Jews "shocked" his "nerves," but then he added that unfortunately he had been forced to act as he did, because of his oath of fidelity and loyalty. It had been his responsibility to deal with the technical aspects of the problem. When the Head of State ordered it and his superiors handed down the order to him, he felt that he was covered; it gave him peace of mind, because the orders enabled him to shift the responsibility to his superiors. Of course he did not mean to say that he had shifted the responsibility to them in fact, but that he had done so in his thoughts, in the deepest part of his heart. "I sensed a kind of Pontius Pilate feeling, for I felt free of all guilt." Who was he "to have [his] own thoughts on the matter."

When Eichmann expressed himself like this, everyone, including the judges, was inclined to believe that he was lying. Hannah Arendt, however, wrote: "And the judges did not believe him, because they were too good, and perhaps also too conscious of the very foundations of their profession, to admit that an average "normal" person, neither feeble-minded nor indoctrinated nor cynical, could be perfectly incapable of telling right from wrong . . ."

She then revealed a man whose conscience had "stopped working," a man who, far from being monstrously dedicated to evil, had become "absolutely incapable of distinguishing between good and evil."

This is what Arendt wrote about Eichmann's execution:

> Adolf Eichmann went to the gallows with great dignity. He had asked for a bottle of red wine and had drunk half of it. He refused the help of the Protestant minister, Reverend William Hull, who offered to read the Bible with him: he had only two more hours to live, and therefore no 'time to waste.' He walked the fifty yards from his cell to the execution chamber calm and erect, with his hands bound behind him. When the guards tied his ankles and knees, he asked them to loosen the bonds so that he could stand straight. 'I don't need that,' he said when the black hood was offered him. He was in complete command of himself, nay, he was more: he was completely himself. Nothing could have demonstrated this more convincingly than the grotesque silliness of his last words. He began by stating emphatically that he was a *Gottgläubiger*, to express in common Nazi fashion that he was no Christian and did not believe in life after death. He then proceeded, 'After a short while, gentlemen, *we shall meet again*. Such is the fate of all men. Long live Germany, long live Argentina, long live Austria. *I shall not forget them.*' In the face of death he had found the cliché used in funeral oratory. Un-

der the gallows, his memory played him the last trick; he was 'elated' and he forgot that this was his own funeral.

It was as though in those last minutes he was summing up the lesson that this long course in human wickedness had taught us – the lesson of the fearsome, word-and-thought-defying *banality of evil.*

Hannah Arendt studied this human symbol for a long time. And the "banality of evil" became for her the principle product of a totalitarian system whose effect was that of "making consciences stop working," making people unable to judge, to distinguish, turning men into bureaucrats. Eichmann was one of many. He had done what was asked of him by the laws of his country, which in turn were justified by reasons of state, without knowing that those laws were unjust. He hadn't even thought about the possible existence of another law higher than the laws of the state, "a law of humanity," a moral law which allowed men to use their judgment.

She wrote:

And just as the law in civilized countries assumes that the voice of conscience tells everybody "Thou shalt not kill," even though man's natural desires and inclinations may at times be murderous, so the law of Hitler's land demanded that the voice of conscience tell everybody: "Thou shalt kill," although the organizers of the massacres knew full well that murder is against the normal desires and inclinations of most people. Evil in the Third Reich had lost the quality by which most people recognize it – the quality of temptation. Many Germans and many Nazis, probably an overwhelming majority of them, must have been tempted *not* to murder, *not* to rob, *not* to let their neighbors go off to their doom (for that the Jews were transported to their doom they knew, of course, even though many of them may not have known the gruesome details), and not to become accomplices in all these crimes by benefiting from them. But, God knows, they had learned how to resist temptation.

To illustrate what she meant by the death of conscience, Arendt quoted a passage from a German writer, Friedrich Reck Malleczeven, who died at the end of the war in a concentration camp. The passage tells the story of a woman Nazi official who went to Bavaria in the summer of 1944 to give a propaganda speech to some farmers. She didn't waste much time talking about "miracle weapons" that would lead to victory, but spoke plainly about the probability of defeat, saying that no good German need be worried because the Führer, "in his great goodness, had prepared for the whole German people a mild death through gassing in case the war should have an unhappy end." To which the writer added this comment, "Oh no, I'm not imagining things, this lovely lady is not a mirage, I saw her with my own eyes; a yellow-skinned female pushing forty, with insane eyes . . . . And what happened? Did these Bavarian peasants at least put her into the local lake to cool off her enthusiastic readiness for death? They did nothing of the sort. They went home, shaking their heads."

Throughout the trial, the attorney for the prosecution would constantly ask the same questions, to each of the one hundred witnesses, "Did the Jews get any help?" and "Why did you not rebel?" The answers were always the same: fear, isolation, resignation, indifference. But, one day, almost by chance, a witness mentioned the name of Anton Schmidt, a sergeant in the German Army who had come across some members of the Jewish underground in Poland and helped them out, providing them with forged documents and army trucks ("and he didn't do it for money"), until he was discovered and executed.

Arendt wrote:

> [H]ush settled over the courtroom; it was as though the
> crowd had spontaneously decided to observe the usual two

minutes of silence in honor of the man named Anton Schmidt. And in those two minutes, which were like a sudden burst of light in the midst of impenetrable, unfathomable darkness, a single thought stood out clearly, irrefutably, beyond question – how utterly different everything would be today in this courtroom, in Israel, in Germany, in all of Europe, and perhaps in all countries of the world, if only more such stories could have been told.

Giorgio Perlasca did not go to Jerusalem to testify in 1961, and in Italy the article that recounted what he had done went completely unnoticed. But if he had taken the witness stand and the prosecutors had asked him, "Signor Perlasca, you were an Italian businessman. You weren't an interested party. You could have escaped from Budapest. Why did you do what you did?" Perlasca would have answered then with the same few words that he repeats today, "I saw people being killed and, quite simply, I couldn't stand it. I had the possibility to do something, and I did what I could. Anyone, in my place, would have done what I did." Maybe he would have added, in his slow Veneto cadence, "In Italy they say that it's the opportunity that makes a man a thief. It made me something else." And his testimony would have been the proof that, even in the most impenetrable darkness, there exists – because it is part of the human spirit – the temptation of the irreducible, fabulous, word-and-thought-defying, "banality of goodness."

Endnote

1. This and other quotations from the Eichmann trial are taken from Hannah Arendt, *Eichmann in Jerusalem: A Report on the Banality of Evil* (New York, Penguin Books), 1994.

Epilogue

Giorgio Perlasca died on the morning of August 15, 1992, of a sudden heart attack in his home in Padua.

Although it was right in the middle of the August holidays, the funeral service was crowded to overflowing. Having heard the news on radio and television or seen it in the newspapers, more than two thousand people showed up at the little church of St. Albertus Magnus, just down the street from Perlasca's house, and the parish priest, Father Esterino Barbiero, felt unprepared. Most of the people in attendance had to stand outside and follow the ceremony by way of the loud speakers set up in the church-yard. In the front rows inside the church, next to family and relatives, sat members of the Jewish community of Padua, representatives from the embassies of Spain, Hungary and Israel, the mayor and, representing the President of the Italian Republic, the Prefect of Padua. Also present, carrying the banner of the city, was a delegation of municipal policemen from Como, Perlasca's home town, which had given him an award.

In front of such a crowd, the pastor declared, it was difficult to find the right words for the burial of such an important man, and so he decided to tell them about a little episode that had happened on the eve of Perlasca's death. The priest was on his way back to the rectory and, walking under the windows of Perlasca's house, he saw Giorgio looking out the window. They said hello to each other, and then Perlasca kept him there for a minute saying, "You know, you priests are a big bunch of liars." "Why do you say that," Father Ernestino asked. "Because whenever someone dies, you're always ready to tell everyone what a good man he was, he was such a good man. Be careful, because if I catch you doing that with me, I'll come back and get you and take you with me."

The church broke out into a wave of laughter. Strange for a funeral, but Perlasca would have appreciated it.

That afternoon back at the house, his son Franco counted up the telegrams that had been sent in memory of his father's work. There were lots of them, including two hundred and two – from Budapest, Jerusalem, Hebron, Haifa, Tel Aviv, Berlin, Frankfurt, Barcelona, New York – from people he had saved.

Since he had been "discovered" in 1987, Giorgio Perlasca had become famous. He had been awarded the Order of the Gold Star by the Hungarian Parliament, named one of the "Just among the Just" and honorary citizen of Israel, honored by the Holocaust Memorial Council of Washington and by the Raoul Wallenberg Committee of New York, named Knight Commander of the Order of Isabella by decree of the King of Spain, Juan Carlos. In Italy, after the publication of this book and a national broadcast of the television show "Mixer" dedicated to his story, Perlasca finally received the official recognition that had been denied him for forty-five years. The President of the Republic, Francesco Cossiga, named him *Commendatore Grand'Ufficiale,* and the government decided to grant him the lifetime annuity under the "Bacchelli Law," which is awarded to eminent citizens living in difficult economic circumstances.

Beginning in 1991, Perlasca was invited to countless ceremonies, debates, and demonstrations. But none of this changed him a bit from the first time I met him. He was always happy to meet people who reminded him of his past life, happy to hear the Spanish or Hungarian language spoken again. He accepted the medals, diplomas and other official symbols of recognition with modesty and displayed them in the little living room in his house. Whenever he and his wife left Padua, she took care to wrap them all up in a big suitcase and give them to a friend for safekeeping, for fear that during their absence thieves might break into the house and steal them.

Perlasca was particularly at ease anytime he could talk to young people and respond to their questions. He always gave them detailed, factual answers, recalling the street names, the cold, the hunger, with serenity, thinking again of the people, especially the children he had managed to save – sad that he had not been able to do more. All of these stories enchanted his audiences. Of all the commemorative plaques he received, his favorite was one given him by the children from the elementary school in his neighborhood that said, "To a man we would like to be like." If he was asked for a comment about the new racism or the new anti-Semitism in Europe, he reacted almost with what seemed a fearful start: "Don't talk about it! Don't publicize it! That's what they want. No, no . . . what happened then cannot happen again." He remained an optimist. A spectator caught between the victims and their persecutors, he had demonstrated that horror can be recognized in time, from the onset of its first symptoms, and that it is possible to oppose it without waiting. With his stories of individual episodes, told with the precision of his memory, he taught that lesson. With respect to current events, however, he confessed his frustration about the energy that he had been able to draw upon as a young man and that now, in his old age, he knew he didn't have anymore. But, stubbornly, he kept on remembering, as he had done, in private, for forty-three years.

The story of Giorgio Perlasca was "saved by a hair." A few more years and it would have been buried or not believed. A few more years and not only its leading protagonist and witness, but all the survivors able to confirm the events, would no longer have been alive. The "international ghetto," the Spanish legation, the banks of the Danube, the safe houses, all would have vanished. Or worse, it might have been declared that they "never existed," just as today, by denying the existence of Auschwitz and desecrating cemeteries, some end-of-the-century Europeans are trying to erase the memory of the 11 million Jews who lived there just a half century ago.

Giorgio Perlasca has had streets and schools named after him, and in Budapest there is a plaque in his honor on the wall of an apartment building in St. Stephen's Park. There are also two plaques in his honor in Padua, one on the steps leading to the front door of the City Hall and one in the park in front of his house.

The times we live in, unfortunately, do not permit me to agree with Perlasca that "what happened then cannot happen again"; too many memories have been stepped on and too many symptoms have reappeared announcing the possibility of a new horror. But it is a pleasure to recall one recent episode of spontaneous reaction. In November 1992, after a series of racist assaults accompanied by the appearance of anti-Semitic graffiti on Rome city streets, a number of store owners in one of the city's popular shopping areas found yellow stickers pasted on their windows with the words "Zionists Out of Italy." Two days later – it was November 9, the anniversary of "Kristallnacht" of 1938 Nazi Germany – tens of thousands of students marched through the streets of Rome in protest. Many of them had sewn on to their clothes or drawn on their faces a yellow star and the words, "All of us are Jews."

Appendix
Random Notes from the Post-War

The Drowned and the Saved in Hungary

Between 1941 and 1945, 565,000 of the 825,000 people considered to be Jews within the territory of "Greater Hungary," or
Hungary prior to the Treaty of Trianon, died in the Holocaust.
About 260,000 survived. In January 1945, some 69,000 Jews
were found alive in the Budapest ghetto and another 25,000 in
the "safe houses" of the "international ghetto." It has been calculated that another 25,000 managed to find a safe hiding place in
and around the Hungarian capital. Several thousand survived in
the safe houses of the International Red Cross. Of those who
were sent off to forced labor camps or as prisoners of war to the
Soviet Union, about 20,000 returned home. Immediately after
the war, 266 of the 473 pre-war Jewish communities were rees-
tablished. In the following years, however, the great majority of
Jews left the cities and towns in the provinces, and the Jewish
communities there ceased to exist.

Ostjuden

In three months Eichmann's organization deported some

440,000 Jews from eastern Hungary ("*Ostjuden*"), mostly to Auschwitz. A few thousand of them managed to survive. Among them was Elie Wiesel, a sixteen year old from the town of Sziget in Transylvania. Deported with his family to Birkenau, Auschwitz and finally to Buchenwald, he was rescued from death by the Allied advance, but his relatives all died. Wiesel moved to France and then to New York and has written numerous books (one in particular, *Night* [1958], is about his deportation from his home town) about the persecution of the Jews. Wiesel was awarded the Nobel Prize for Peace in 1986 "for his defense of human dignity and for his symbolic representation of the cause of all oppressed peoples."

Eyewitness accounts of the deportations from Transylvania have also been gathered by a Hungarian writer living in Italy, Edith Bruck (*Lettera alla madre* [Garzanti, 1988]).

On the *Ostjuden* and their assimilation in the West see also *Ebrei erranti* by Joseph Roth, written in 1927 (Adelphi, 1985). One of the young Hungarian Jews, Arthur Koestler, born in Budapest in 1905, has left us in his books the insights of a literary and political precursor: *The Sleepwalkers* on emigration to Palestine in the 1920s and *Darkness at Noon* on Stalinism.

The photographs found by the girl from Bilke were published in *The Auschwitz Album*, edited by Peter Hellman, Lili Meier and Beate Klarsfield (New York: Random House, 1981).

Eighteenth-century travelers' accounts of the Hungarian *puszta* are contained in *What They Saw in Hungary* (Budapest, 1988).

What Happened to Them after the War

Hannah Arendt was born in Hanover in 1906 to a Jewish family from Konigsberg. She studied with Heidegger and Karl Jaspers. In 1941 she moved to the United States, where she wrote *The Origins of Totalitarianism* (1951) and *The Human Condition* (1958). She died in 1975. The book *Eichmann in Jerusalem*

(New York, 1963, 1994) was published in Italy with the title *La banalità del male* by Feltrinelli in 1964 and again in 1992. Regarding the controversy provoked by its publication see *Hannah Arendt: For Love of the World*, a biography written by her student, Elisabeth Young-Bruehl.

Angel Sanz Briz left Hungary for Switzerland on December 1, 1944. After the war he became Ambassador to Holland, and later he was appointed Spanish Ambassador to the Holy See. He died in 1978. The State of Israel recognized him as one of the Just among the Just, and a tree was planted in his name on the Avenue of Remembrance in Jerusalem.

Admiral Miklós Horthy left Hungary escorted by the German army on October 16, 1944. He lived in Germany as a quasi-prisoner until the end of the war when he moved to Portugal. He died in Oporto in 1957. He left an autobiography entitled *A Life for Hungary.*

Miklós Horthy, Jr., the Admiral's son, was kidnapped by the SS under the command of Major Skorzeny on October 15, 1944, and deported to the concentration camp at Mauthausen, where he was saved by Allied troops in 1945. Count Miklós Kalláy, the Hungarian Prime Minister until March 1944 who had attempted to negotiate a separate peace with the Allies, was detained in the same camp and saved together with Horthy, Jr.

Rudolph Kasztner, President of the Zionist organization in Budapest who negotiated with the SS, offering money for the lives of a list of Hungarian Jews even as he knew (since May 1944) about the "total deportation" plan drawn up by the Nazis, continued to negotiate with them in Austria and Switzerland until the end of the war. In August 1947, he signed an affidavit in favor of Kurt Becher, one of Eichmann's deputies. Brought to trial in Jerusalem in 1954, he was told by Judge Benjamin Halevi that he "had sold his soul to the devil." In 1957 Kasztner was assassinated on a street in Tel Aviv. The following year the Supreme Court of Israel rehabilitated his memory.

Ottó Komoly, a leader of the Zionist organization in Budapest, President of the local committee of the International Red Cross and member of the Jewish Council, was killed on January 1, 1945, by militants of the Arrow Cross Party. His diary of his activities and meetings between August 21 and September 16, 1944, was published in *Hungarian Jewish Studies* (New York, 1972).

Béla Kun, the leader of the Bolshevik-inspired Republic of the Councils which held power in Hungary for 113 days in 1919, fled Budapest on July 31 of that year for Vienna. After a brief period of internment, he went to the Soviet Union, where he became a leader of the Communist International. In 1937, in the middle of the Stalinist purges, he was put on trial by the Presidium of the Communist International. He disappeared shortly after the trial and, according to unofficial sources, died in November 1939.

György Lukács, Marxist philosopher and Minister of Education in Kun's government. When the Republic fell, Lukács sought refuge in several countries before going finally to the USSR. After 1945 he was given the Chair of Esthetics at the University of Budapest, and in 1956 he became Minister of Education in the government of Imre Nagy. When the revolt was put down, Lukács was put in prison and then deported to Romania. Some years later he was allowed to return to Hungary, where he died in 1971.

Ferenc Molnár, author of the famous *The Paul Street Boys* as well as numerous plays and theater pieces, left Hungary in 1935 and established himself in the United States four years later. In his autobiographical book, *Farewell, My Love,* he tells the story of a Hungarian writer who escapes from Europe as it is about to be thrown into chaos by the spread of Nazism. His play, *Liliom,* was transformed into a Broadway musical (*Carousel*). His books were banned in Hungary and burned in the square in Budapest in the spring of 1944 after being branded contrary to "Magyar culture." The Molnár family archives were destroyed in 1944. Molnár died in New York in 1952. Places and settings used by Molnár in his books can still be seen on the present-day Paul Street, although it is not included on the tour guides' customary route.

Monsignor Angelo Roncalli, Apostolic Delegate in Turkey and Greece from 1935 until the end of 1944, was the author of numerous and timely letters of warning about the extermination of the Jews then in progress in Central Europe. He even told the German Ambassador in Ankara, Franz von Papen, that he knew that "millions of Jews are being sent to Poland to be killed" (July 1943). Also in 1943 he used his offices to make it possible for a steamship carrying a cargo of Jewish children who had escaped deportation to get through the mesh of the German blockade and make its way to Palestine, and he worked constantly and effectively in support of efforts to save both Polish and Hungarian Jews.

From 1945 to 1953 he was Papal Nuncio in France, and in 1953 he became Patriarch of Venice, where he served until 1958, the year he succeeded Pius XII as Pope, taking the name John XXIII. Five months after his election he issued a decree eliminating from the liturgy for Good Friday the word "wicked" in reference to the Jews. In 1962 he gave his blessing to the faithful coming out of the synagogue in Rome after their weekly prayer service. The Second Vatican Council, despite some protest, eliminated the accusation of the Jews as "deicides" and explicitly condemned anti-Semitism.

He died in Rome in 1963. In October 1964, his encyclical

"Pacem in Terris" became the first papal document to be translated into Hebrew.

Francisco Franco, the laconic savior. Although it is seldom mentioned, Franco's Spain played a decidedly superior role to that of the Allied democracies in the rescue of European Jews. The figures vary from 30,000 to 60,000. According to Chaim U. Lipschitz (*Franco, Spain, the Jews and the Holocaust* [New York: Ktav Publishing House, 1984]), the number of Jews brought to safety was around 45,000. Rescue operations were effected principally through the "Pyrenean route," which provided safe passage to some 28,000 Jews from all over Europe. From there, some of them went on to Lisbon, the principal neutral port and point of communication with the Allied countries. Other rescue operations were carried out, upon specific and "energetic" requests from the Generalissimo, by the Spanish diplomatic corps in a number of countries. France, Hungary, Romania and Greece were the countries where these efforts proved most effective.

An ally of Hitler and Mussolini, who had helped him take power at the end of the Civil War against the Republicans, Franco declared in 1940 that Spain would remain "nonbelligerent" in World War II. For the entire duration of the conflict he assured Hitler of his support in principle, but he refused to take part in any military actions, which Berlin continued to request with ever more urgency.

Persecuted by the Inquisition beginning in 1478, the Sephardic Jews (*Sepharad* is the Hebrew word for Spain) were expelled from the country in 1492 and were dispersed in many countries of Europe and North Africa. Four centuries later their return was favored by Kings Alphonso XII and XIII, who considered the expulsion a "black page" in Spanish history. In 1924 a law promoted by the dictator Miguel Primo de Rivera granted Spanish citizenship to Jews of Sephardic ancestry scattered around the world. The "Rivera Law" was the legal basis for

Franco's activity on behalf of the Jews during the Second World War.

In the post-war period, the theme of Franco's relationship to the Jews was largely ignored. Franco's only interview on the subject (conducted by Chaim Lipschutz in 1970) was very disappointing. The Generalissimo limited himself to confirmation of the figures and laconically explained his attitude as an "elementary sense of justice and Christian charity." Some historians have brought to light some other possible motivations, including Franco's intuition about the final outcome of the war, the desire to reestablish political and commercial contacts with Jews in the Mediterranean, his wish to secure himself a noble place in history, and the possibility of his own Jewish ancestry.

In 1992, on the occasion of the five-hundredth anniversary of the discovery of America (but also of the expulsion of the Jews), the Spanish government announced new measures in favor of Spanish citizenship for the descendants of Sephardic Jews.

Monsignor Angelo Rotta, finished his service as Nuncio in Budapest and returned to the Vatican, where he worked in the office of the Secretary of State until his death in 1963.

Otto Skorzeny, the SS Colonel who freed Mussolini from his hotel-prison in Gran Sasso (September 12, 1943), and who kidnapped Miklós Horthy, Jr. (October 15, 1944), was captured by American troops in Germany in August 1945, and sent to a prisoner-of-war camp. He managed to escape and fled to Spain where he died of cancer in 1975. In 1989 an Israeli monthly, *Matara,* revealed that in 1962 the Mossad, the Israeli Secret Service, had contacted the colonel and, in exchange for his continued safety, obtained the chance to infiltrate some of their agents among the ex-Nazis that Skorzeny had placed in service to President Nasser of Egypt. In this way, the Israelis were able to direct the dismantling of Egypt's radar and missile defense system, an operation which allowed them, in 1967, to wipe out the entire Egyptian air force within hours after the outbreak of the Six Day War.

Ferenc Szálasi, József Gera, Gábor Kemény, Gábor and *Ernö Vajna* were among the leaders of the Arrow Cross Party who took refuge in Austria. Captured by the Allied army, they were brought back to Hungary and were tried, convicted and hanged in November 1945.

Gennaro Verolino, secretary at the Nuncio in Budapest, later served as Apostolic Nuncio in several countries in Latin America.

Raoul Wallenberg, the envoy of the King of Sweden who operated in Budapest from July 1944, until the Red Army arrived in the city, disappeared on January 18, 1945. Considered one of the heroes of the Second World War and the architect of a rescue operation that saved thousands of Hungarian Jews, Wallenberg disappeared during the first days of the Soviet occupation of the Hungarian capital. In the decades since then, there have been many hypotheses concerning his destiny, including – as believed by his family – that he was still alive and imprisoned in the Soviet Union. The authorities in Moscow, in response to the many requests for information, gave a number of different versions of events. For many years it was said that the "Soviet government knows absolutely nothing about him." In 1987, however, the Soviet Foreign Minister gave Wallenberg's step-sister and step-brother, who had come to Moscow from Stockholm, his diplomatic passport. On that occasion it was explained that Wallenberg had died in July 1947, in Lubianka, the KGB prison, of "cardiac failure." His arrest and imprisonment were considered by the Soviets to have been a "tragic error," caused by the chaotic conditions in Budapest during the final days of the war.

Giorgio Perlasca was one of the last people to see Wallenberg alive. He recalls that, at the beginning of January 1945, Wallenberg made a request for protection from the Spanish legation, and he remembers going, on January 18, to an appointment with Wallenberg in a neighborhood in Budapest that was still a theater for combat operations. Though he has no proof of this, Perlasca believes it quite probable that Wallenberg was killed accidentally by a stray bullet during one of those final battles. Among the many publications about Wallenberg, see the book by Frederick E. Werbell and Thurston Clarke, *Lost Hero: The Mystery of Raoul Wallenberg* (New York: McGraw-Hill, 1982).

The State of Things

Property. The Manfred Weiss industrial complex, the bastion of blue-collar support for the Arrow Cross Party from 1940 to 1944, was sold in June 1944, to the SS, after a secret negotiation, in exchange for safe passage for forty-six members of the owners' families. After the war it was returned, for a brief time only, to its original owners. It was expropriated and nationalized with the rise to power of the Communist Party in 1948. Ferenc Chorin, who negotiated the 1944 sale, died in the United States in 1964. In 1956 the workers of the ex-Manfred Weiss were among the vanguard in the revolt against Stalinism.

The Eszterházy family, symbols of nobility and large landownership, held on to their possessions in Austria after the war, but those in Hungary were confiscated by the Communist government. In Hungary today, two sons of the famous landowner are very popular. Péter Eszterházy is a writer, and Marton Eszterházy, a soccer player, has played for years as the center forward of the Panatinaikos team in Athens and has also been a member of the Hungarian national team.

Racial Laws in Italy. The Italian racial laws were handed down on July 14, 1938, with the publication of the "scientist's manifesto" which declared that the Jews were biologically ex-

{155}

traneous to the national community. On August 22, the Minister of the Interior ordered a census which established at 58,412 the number of Italian and foreign Jews resident in Italy (the census followed the principle of race rather than religious faith and included 11,756 converts and non-Jewish children of mixed marriages). On September 2 of the same year Italian citizenship was revoked for foreign Jews who had obtained it after 1919, and a decree was issued expelling them from the realm. On November 15, a decree expelled Jewish professors and students from the schools and established a cap on the amount of property that could be held by Jews. On November 17, marriages between Jews and non-Jews were prohibited. The same decree excluded Jews from military service, the public administration and membership in the Fascist Party. On February 9, 1939, it was established that property owned by Jews in excess of the limits set down in the law of the preceding November had to be transferred to the *Ente di Gestione e Liquidazione Immobiliare* (Agency for the Management and Liquidation of Real Property). On July 13, 1939, a special commission was created, as part of an Aryanization program, which could declare arbitrarily that a Jew was not a Jew. Between 1938 and 1942 dozens of circulars and regulations were issued by the *Direzione Generale per la Demografia e la Razza* (The General Office for Demography and Race), part of the Ministry of Internal Affairs, prohibiting a huge number of activities that were part of everyday life: Street vending and bookselling were prohibited as were the publication of obituaries, ownership of a radio, access to libraries, membership in sporting clubs, cultural associations and so on.

After the fall of fascism on July 25, 1943, the racial laws were not abrogated. Nor were they abrogated after the signing of the Armistice on September 8, 1943. Abrogation did not come until the issuance of Royal Decree Laws 25 and 26 of January 1944, which did not go into effect until October 5, 1944.

In 1938, there were 47,252 Jews in Italy. On July 25, 1943,

there were 40,157, including some 6,500 foreign Jews. Some 8,566 Jews were deported from Italy and the Dodecanese Islands, 7,557 of whom died. The deportations reached their peak in the autumn-winter of 1943.

Information and accounts of the deportation of Jews from Italy are contained in *Il libro della memoria* (*The Book of Memory*) by Liliana Picciotto Fargion (Mursia, 1991). Essays on the racial laws can be found in *La legislazione anti-ebraica in Italia ed in Europa*, Chamber of Deputies, 1988. For a general overview of the subject, Renzo De Felice, *Storia degli ebrei italiani sotto il fascismo* (*The History of Italian Jews Under Fascism*) Einaudi, 1972; Susan Zuccotti, *Italians and the Holocaust*, Basic Books, 1987; *The Italian Refugees: Rescue of Jews During the Holocaust*, edited by Ivo Herzer, The Catholic University of America Press, 1989; *L'abrogazione delle leggi razziali in Italia* (1943–1987), edited by Mario Toscano. An in-depth study of the application of the anti-Semitic laws and regulations in Turin from 1938 to 1945 is provided by *L'ebreo in oggetto* (*The Jew in Question*), edited by Fabio Levi (Silvio Zamorani editore, 1991).

Racial Laws in Hungary. An account of the Parliamentary proceedings concerning the three Hungarian anti-Semitic laws is contained in *Rassegna d'Ungheria* (*Hungarian Review*), a monthly periodical directed by Béla Gády and Rodolfo Mosca (secretary of the Institute of Italian Culture in Budapest), Library of the Italian Senate. Analysis and interpretations of the laws are provided by Istvan Bibo, already cited.

Coincidences. By a sheer quirk of fate, during the period that the Giorgio Perlasca story was being rediscovered, a book came out which dealt with an analogous subject. *The Bellarosa Connection*, by Saul Bellow (Penguin Books, 1989), tells the story of a Jewish boy, Harry Fonstein, who is saved from the Nazis by a clandestine group financed by the Broadway impresario, Billy Rose. Feinstein then spends the rest of his life trying, without success, to meet his savior and thank him. The story told in the film *Music Box* is just the opposite of Perlasca's experience. Based on a story by Deborah Chiel, directed by Costa Gavras and starring Jessica Lange and Armin Mueller-Stahl, *Music Box* is the story of a Hungarian-American in Chicago, accused after forty years of having committed atrocities during the Nazi years. His lawyer daughter defends him and wins an acquittal, but then, on a trip to Budapest, she finds a music box with the proof of her father's guilt and turns him in to the federal investigators.

Budapest in Hollywood. A large number of Hungarian Jews, emigrants fleeing from poverty and discrimination, found a place among the pioneers of American cinema. Among them were: the producers Alexander Korda, Adolph Zukor (Paramount), William Fox (Twentieth Century Fox), Morris Kohn, and the director George Cukor.

"Prevented from entering the ranks of power in American society by the main road, they created an empire of their own, colonizing the American imagination to such an extent that the country identified itself in large part with its movies." This is the thesis of a brilliant essay by Neal Gabler, *An Empire of Their Own: How the Jews Invented Hollywood* (New York: Crown, 1988).

Some of the great Hungarian film actors of the past are Bela Lugosi (who identified so completely with the role of Dracula that he asked to be buried in a coffin just like the Count's), Eva Bartok (today a resident of Polynesia), and Zsa Zsa Gábor, who was elected, in some unknown year, Miss Hungary.

Hollywood in Budapest. A Conversation with Tony Curtis. Born in New York, in the Bronx, in 1925 with the name of Bernard Schwartz, the American actor Tony Curtis has now become one of the most steadfast supporters of the effort to preserve the memory of the Hungarian Jews. In the name of his father, Emanuel Schwartz, who emigrated to the United States from Hungary in 1920, Curtis chairs and finances the "Emanuel Schwartz Foundation," an institution whose goals are to save the spiritual and material heritage of the Jews of Hungary, to encourage the teaching of Hebrew in the schools, and to promote Hebrew summer schools.

The father of six children, including the actress Jamie Lee (*Trading Places, A Fish Called Wanda*), Tony Curtis has acted in one hundred and fifty films. He splits his time between Hollywood and the Hawaiian Islands. A few years ago he presented a show of paintings and drawings that he had done throughout his career and signed with the pseudonym Gauguin Schwartz. One of them, "The Legend," was a portrait of Marilyn Monroe whom he starred with in 1959 in Billy Wilder's *Some Like It Hot*.

Tony Curtis had this to say about his current commitments:

> As a child in the Bronx, they thought of me as a foreigner in America. I spoke English with a terribly thick accent, just like all the other Hungarian immigrants who continued to use their own language at home with their families. My father, Emanuel Schwartz, was a Jew from the town of Mateszalka, which today is on the border with Romania. But other branches of my family have their roots in other parts of Europe. There are the Kertész, the Taubs, and even an Italian branch, the Vittucci. I think you could say I'm a kind of European concentrate, but I didn't know about any of this when I was young. I did my military service in the Navy, and if you asked me what I knew back then about Hitler's Europe, I'd tell you nothing. I was a very naive young man. I started learning these things later, when I began working in Hollywood, where there has always been a big Hungarian community, and when I started acting in Europe. That was when I started to get interested in finding out about my family's history. So, a few years ago when Mr. Ándor Weiss came to me and asked if I would finance

the rehabilitation of the Dohány Street Synagogue in Budapest, I was very happy to do it. I remembered what my father used to say to me. When he would go to the capital from his home in the country the first thing he would do was go to pray at the Temple on Dohány Street and then at the one on Kazinczy Street. When I was in Hungary and I walked down those stone streets I thought, 'These are the same stones that my father used to walk on, and nobody is taking care of them.' That's why I think it's right that I give some money to keep those places, those monuments, from being destroyed. The project is coming along very well. The Foundation is working directly with the Hungarian government.

I've read a lot of Hungarian history and about what happened there during the war. I've also heard about Signor Perlasca. I'll be in Budapest next July 1992, for the unveiling of a monument in the Dohány Street synagogue dedicated to all those who worked to save the Hungarian Jews. It's dedicated to Giorgio Perlasca too. I hope to meet him then.

Asked for his professional opinion about a hypothetical screenplay for a film on Perlasca, Tony Curtis didn't have any doubts:

It should definitely be an action film: a man alone against everyone in a destroyed city; a solitary man fighting against silence and indifference. It might seem like his story is not very easy to tell because it takes place in two different time periods: first, during the war and now, almost a half century later. That's why the screenplay should be written to show the events of the past in their most dramatic and immediate aspects. If it succeeded in rendering the climate of fear and shame, the sense of guilt that there was back then, then it would be possible to understand why the silence about it has lasted for so many years, and to appreciate the greatness of this Italian gentleman.

Sources

The two most important texts for the study of the Holocaust in Hungary are *The Politics of Genocide: The Holocaust in Hungary* by Randolph L. Braham, (New York: Columbia University Press, 1981) and *Black Book on the Martyrdom of Hungarian Jewry* (Central European Times Publishing Co., 1948), by Jenö Lévai. The Holocaust in Hungary also receives in-depth treatment in *The Destruction of the European Jews* by Raul Hilberg (London, 1985), and *The Final Solution* by Arno J. Mayer (New York: Pantheon, 1990). Reflections on events in Hungary with particular attention for anti-Semitism can be found in *Misère des petits Etats de l'Est*, by Istvan Bilbo (Paris: Harmattan, 1986).

Information on the attitude of the Allied Powers with regard to the Nazi persecution of the Jews can be found in *The Abandonment of the Jews: America and the Holocaust 1941–1945*, by David S. Wymann (New York: Pantheon Books, 1984).

In Randolph Braham's book on the Hungarian Holocaust, Perlasca is cited in the chapter about the activities of the neutral embassies present in Budapest:

> Sanz Briz and his colleagues returned to Spain shortly after Szálasi was inaugurated. Leadership at the Spanish legation was taken over by Giorgio (Jorge) Perlasca. An anti-fascist Italian, he had already been a frequent visitor

to the legation (he had a personal friend there). His assumption of duties was therefore not viewed with suspicion by the lower rank personnel or by the Nyilas Ministry of Foreign Affairs, which recognized him as the new chargé d'affaires. Perlasca and his colleagues issued some 3,000 protective passes. Like the other protected Jews, the Spanish protected ones were relocated into the international ghetto after November 15th. Early in January 1945, they were transferred into the large ghetto.

The Germans, apparently unaware of Perlasca's personal role, were quite disturbed over the Spanish legation's rescue activities. The accusatory reports on the Spanish government's involvement in the rescue of Hungarian Jews disturbed the Germans in Budapest, Berlin, and Madrid. On October 13th, Thadden reported that, on the initiative of the Americans, the Spanish government was ready to issue visas to 2,000 Jews. About ten days later, Ballensiefen, the SS propaganda expert in Budapest, informed Rolf Günther, Eichmann's deputy in Berlin, that "the Spanish Legation in Budapest had made an offer to the Jewish Council to protect Jewish orphans of 14 to 16 years of age. During the death marches, Veesenmayer reported (November 13) that the Spaniards requested exit visas for additional Hungarian Jews having family relationships in Spain" (*The Politics of Genocide: The Holocaust in Hungary*, vol. 2, pp. 1092–93).

In 1989 the Hungarian writer Elek László published, in homage to Perlasca, a collection of documents and tributes in a book with the title *Az olasz Wallenberg* (The Italian Wallenberg), (Budapest: Szécheny Kiado KFT, 1989).

A nice portrait of life during the war in a Jewish neighborhood in Budapest is provided by the book, *Homage to the Eighth District* by Giorgio and Nicola Pressburger (translated by Gerald Moore). Three later books by Giorgio Pressburger, *L'elefante verde* (The Green Elephant), *The Law of the White Spaces* (translated by Piers Spence), and *Il sussurro della grande voce* (The Whisper of the Great Voice) are set in the same location.

Sources

There are only a few Italian books dealing with the history of Hungary during the Second World War. One of them is *I falsi fascismi. Ungheria, Jugoslavia, Romania 1919–1945* by Mariano Ambri (Rome: Jouvence, 1980). For a rightist perspective see Michele Rallo's *L'epoca delle rivoluzioni nazionali: Austria, Cecoslovakia, Ungheria* (Rome: Edizioni Settimo Sigillo, 1987) and Ferenc Szàlasi, Discorso agli intellettuali, Quaderni del Veltro (Padua: edizioni AR, 1977). Ambassador Filippo Anfuso's *Roma-Berlino-Salò* by Filippo Anfuso (Garzanti, 1950) is an autobiographical account.